First published in the United States of America in 2026 by

Rizzoli Universe, a Division of

Rizzoli International Publications, Inc.

49 West 27th Street, New York, NY 10001

rizzoliusa.com

Conceived, designed, and produced by Copyright Editions, 25 rue Pierre Nicole, 75005 Paris, France

copyright-editions.net

© 2026 Copyright Editions

First edition published in 2014 and revised in 2017. Second edition published in 2020.

For Rizzoli

Publisher: Charles Miers

Editor: Klaus Kirschbaum

Assistant Editor: Emily Ligniti

Managing Editor: Lynn Scrabis

For Copyright Editions

Editor: Nicolas Marçais

Art Direction: Philippe Marchand

Author: Bernard Lions

Translation: Roland Glasser

Shirt Design: Stan Moreau

ISBN: 978-0-7893-4632-2

Library of Congress Control Number: 2025946185

Printed in Bosnia & Herzegovina

2026 2027 2028 / 10 9 8 7 6 5 4 3 2 1

The authorized representative in the EU for product safety and compliance is

Mondadori Libri S.p.A., via Gian Battista Vico 42, Milan, Italy, 20123

mondadori.it

Visit us online

Facebook.com/RizzoliNewYork

Instagram.com/RizzoliBooks

Youtube.com/user/RizzoliNY

FSC

www.fsc.org

MIX

Paper | Supporting
responsible forestry

FSC® C118234

1000
football
shirts

FROM VINTAGE CLASSICS
TO THE LATEST RELEASES

Bernard Lions

Foreword by
Carlo Ancelotti

RIZZOLI
UNIVERSE

I was Tagnin. Dreaming of Di Stéfano.

I was not as chubby as I am now. Back then my heart was clearly visible under a thin layer of skin. More than feel it, you could see it pounding. We're talking about the beating heart of a six-year-old child who had just been given his first football shirt. Pure emotion. Even then I was called Carletto, but that day I was not Ancelotti. I was Tagnin; defensive midfielder who, at Prater stadium in Vienna only a few months before, had taken the legendary, luminary Alfredo Di Stéfano out of the European cup final. The shirt was that of Inter, my first love, overwhelming passion and memorable better half (or rather my better third, because my size has over time become cumbersome, invading other people's space...) and the shirt that, for work, I had to leave behind.

Made from a heavy fabric, the shirt was so hot that it overwhelmed me in the winter and in the summer risked hospitalizing me for suffocation, yet it was my formula for happiness. A suit of armour against everyone and everything. Soaked to capacity during lightning storms and abominable when the sun was out. Its fibres overlapped, running, rebelling, and tangling around me. Maybe I scratched, but I kept smiling, because you cannot be allergic to beauty.

The lines were very thick, black as the fear that overwhelmed opponents, and as blue as the sky, and the secret was right there: to compose the best stories you do not need an infinite number of pages, a few lines are sufficient. Those lines. Some sweet emotions can also be written vertically. They had not yet added the numbers, nor the names to be stuck on the back, and it was all so perfect: a diamond, to be such, must remain raw. Any impurities will ruin its elegance.

That for me was the shirt and will remain so forever. To be used during the games of the imagination, on a field of dirt in which I saw the finely cut grass of the San Siro. Surrounded by the purest thoughts. As a player first and then as a manager, the colours would change, the boundaries also, the prospects as well, but the first love is never forgotten. Not a collector's item, simply a piece of my heart. I was Tagnin. Dreaming of Di Stéfano.

Carlo ANCELOTTI
Manager of Brazil national team, 2025–
(Former player for Parma, Roma, and AC Milan, and
former manager of Reggiana, Parma, Juventus FC,
AC Milan, Chelsea FC, Paris Saint-Germain,
Bayern Munich, Napoli, Everton FC, and Real Madrid)

Contents

Notts County FC, the oldest football club in the world still playing at a professional level. The club was founded in 1862. (Group photograph taken in 1905.)

Roger Milla couldn't help himself. When the final whistle signaled the end of Cameroon's historic win over Argentina in Italia 90's opening game, the 38-year-old Indomitable Lion chased after Maradona and asked for his jersey. With the shock of defeat still fresh, the Argentina icon offered up his stripes gladly, with a smile, draping Milla's green shirt across his own shoulders.

Some shirts remain forever connected to the great ones who wore them—Alfredo Di Stéfano in the pure white of Madrid, Maradona in the light blue of Napoli, Cruyff in his bright orange, Zidane all in royal, blazing blue. Even for the greatest players, a football jersey stirs emotions. On pitches across the world, players swap them with opponents. Sometimes after a glorious victory, sometimes in the doldrums of defeat, and sometimes even at half-time with the game still in the balance! These shirts often end up in frames, behind glass, and hanging in homes, cherished symbols of past battles.

The sight of players swapping shirts at the end of a match is now commonplace, but that was not the case until May 31, 1931. The French, delighted to have beaten the English for the first time in ten years, asked if they could keep their opponents' jerseys as a souvenir of the match. This sporting behaviour later gained worldwide acceptance when Pelé and Bobby Moore swapped shirts at the final whistle of Brazil's hard-fought 1–0 win over England on June 7, 1970 at the World Cup in Mexico. While swapping shirts at the end of a game is now customary, taking off a shirt during a game to celebrate a goal or for almost any other reason is considered unsportsmanlike behaviour and prohibited by FIFA.

Of course, there are some memorable exceptions. When Chelsea played against Reading on October 14, 2006 both goalkeeper Cech and substitute goalkeeper Cudicini left the field with injuries. Captain and central defender John Terry put on a goalkeeper's jersey and finished the game between the uprights. On April 13, 1996, Sir Alex Ferguson, down 3–0 against Southampton, made his Manchester United players switch shirts at half-time blaming the kit's grey colour for the team's poor performance. It almost worked. They got one goal back but still ended up losing the game.

Shirts do so much more than tell the history of football. They speak of legend. They stand for entire eras, stoking memories and dreams of impossible matches and unforgettable teams.

White is no longer cursed

THE SELEÇÃO BEGAN THEIR COPA AMÉRICA 2019 IN WHITE, A COLOUR THAT HAD BEEN CURSED FOR NEARLY SEVENTY YEARS. IT DID NOT STOP THEM FROM WINNING, HOWEVER.

When the Brazilian Football Federation (CBF) announced that the Seleção would celebrate the centenary of their first victory in the Copa América by playing the opening match against Bolivia in white (3–0), the Brazilians' blood suddenly ran cold. Although white had been the original colour of Brazil's shirt, it had been cursed since July 16, 1950, when Uruguay deprived them of final victory in "their" FIFA World Cup (1–2). This traumatic defeat went down in history as "the Maracanaçao" ("the Agony at Maracanã"). Neymar's right-ankle injury during the final preparation match against Qatar (2–0 on June 6, 2019) seemed to confirm this jinx.

Despite playing without their number 10, Brazil managed finally to drive the curse away by beating Peru in the final (3–1 on July 7, 2019). That evening, the Seleção wore retro *auriverde* (gold and green) uniforms, with a green polo collar, honouring the victory of 1989, which was also won at home. Green symbolises the Amazonian forests, and yellow, the gold deposits of a country that has won four of its five World Cups with the *Canarinha* (Little Canary) kit, having won its first in 1958, in the color blue, in Sweden.

BRASIL

11
GLOBAL HONOURS
5 FIFA World Cups
4 FIFA Confederations Cups
2 Olympic Games

9
CONTINENTAL HONOURS
9 Copas América

2002
World Cup–
winning jersey

Pelé, number 10 by chance

Players have not always performed with a number on their back, let alone a name. Introduced during the 1930s in England, systematic numbering was formalised by FIFA at the 1954 World Cup. And it was not until the 1958 tournament in Sweden that the number 10 came to symbolise the team's most creative player, due to a 17-year-old debutant named Pelé and a bureaucratic error by the Brazilian FA. Before the start of the competition, Brazil's football powers sent in the list of selected players, as required, but they forgot to allocate specific jersey numbers to the players. A FIFA delegate from Uruguay took charge, rather obliviously handing the number 3 shirt to the first-choice goalkeeper, Gilmar, and the 10 to the hitherto unknown Pelé. Injured in the run-up to the global gathering, Pelé made his first appearance during the third match against USSR and went on to score six goals in four matches. He scored three times in the 5–2 win over France during the semifinal and twice over Sweden in the final, Brazil winning again 5–2. And so the legend of the number 10 was born. By chance.

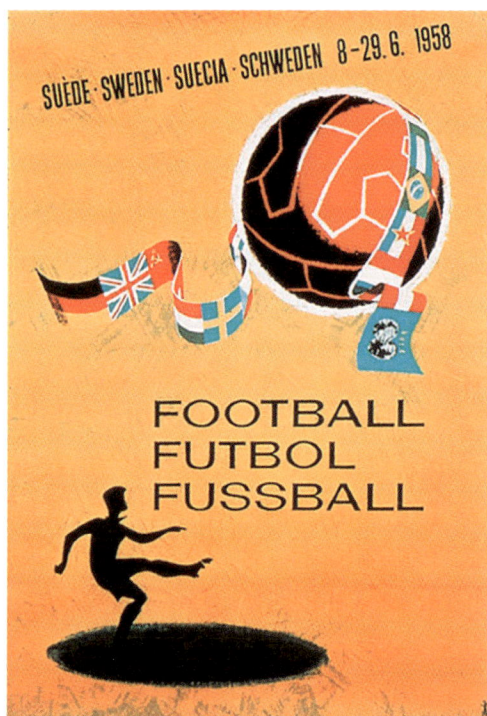

SUÈDE · SWEDEN · SUECIA · SCHWEDEN 8-29.6. 1958

FOOTBALL
FUTBOL
FUSSBALL

MEXICO CITY (MEXICO), AZTECA STADIUM
JUNE 21, 1970
Pelé celebrates in Jairzinho's arms after heading Brazil into a lead in the World Cup final against Italy.

Picture credits

p. 1 : © Actionplus/Icon Sport (h) ; © Conteudo/Icon Sport (b) ; p. 6 : © PA Images/Icon Sport ; p. 7 : © Oleksiewicz/Newspix/Icon Sport ; pp. 8-9 : © Central Press/Getty Images ; p. 14 : © fifa.com ; p. 15 : © Ullstein Bild/Roger-Viollet ; pp. 18-19 : © D.R. ; p. 22 : © Allsport/Getty Images ; p. 23 : © Streubel/Bongarts/Getty Images ; pp. 26-27 : © DPA ; pp. 30-31 : © Botterill/Getty Images ; p. 33 : © Michele Finessi/AFLO/Presse Sports ; p. 39 : © Thomas/Getty Images ; pp. 40-41 : © D.R. ; p. 47 : © L'EQUIPE/Presse Sports (hg) ; © DE MARTIGNAC ALAIN/Presse Sports (hd) ; © SEGUIN FRANCK/Presse Sports (bg) ; © LAHALLE/Presse Sports (bd) ; pp. 48-49 : © Actionplus/Icon Sport ; p. 55 : © Newspix/Icon Sport ; p. 61 : © Mutsu Kawamori/AFLO/Presse Sports ; p. 67 : © Botterill/Allsport/Getty Images ; p. 73 : © Stickland/Allsport/Getty Images (hg) ; © Cannon/Getty Images (hd) ; © Stewart/ Allsport/Getty Images (bg) ; © Thomas/Getty Images (bd) ; p. 79 : © Liverani/Icon Sport (hg) ; © Thomas/Getty Images (hd) ; © Thomas/Getty Images (bg) ; © Liverani/Icon Sport (bd) ; p. 85 : © Szwarc/Bongarts/Getty Images ; p. 91 : © Szwarc/Bongarts/ Getty Images ; p. 97 : © Le Gouic/Icon Sport ; p. 103 : © SUSA/Icon Sport ; p. 109 : © Spi/Icon Sport ; p. 115 : © UNC Athletic Communications Archives (hg) ; © Grimm/Getty Images (hd) ; © Beck/Sports Illustrated/Getty Images (bg) ; © Bildbyran/Icon Sport (bd) ; p. 121 : © Oscar J. Barroso/AFP7 /Presse Sports (h) ; © PAPON/Presse Sports (b) ; p. 127 : © ATSUSHI TOKUMARU/ AFLO/Presse Sports ; p. 132 : © Zabala/Photoshot/Icon Sport ; p. 133 : © Bancet/Icon Sport ; p. 139 : © Presse Sports (hg) ; © PAPON/Presse Sports (hd) ; © Alfonso Cannavacciuolo/IPP/Presse Sports (b) ; pp. 142-143 : © RICHIARDI/Presse Sports ; p. 146 : © Marcarian/Reuters ; p. 153 : © Sven Hoppe/PICTURE ALLIANCE/Presse Sports ; p. 159 : © Cameron/Sportimage/Icon Sport ; p. 165 : © Rue des Archives/AGIP ; p. 171 : © Allsport/Getty Images ; p. 177 : © Michele Finessi/AFLO/Presse Sports ; p. 182 : © Photoshot/Icon Sport ; p. 183 : © Action Images/Presse Sports ; p. 189 : © Hangst/Witters/Presse Sports ; p. 195 : © Motivio/ dpa-Zentralbild/PICTURE ALLIANCE/Presse Sports ; p. 201 : © WilfriedWitters/WITTERS/Presse Sports ; p. 206 : © D.R. ; p. 207 : © Rys/Bongarts/Getty Images ; p. 213 : © Oscar J. Barroso/AFP7/Presse Sports ; p. 219 : © Gambarini/DPA/Corbis ; p. 225 : © Simon Stacpoole/OFFSIDE/Presse Sports ; p. 231 : © Ricardo Larreina/AFP7/Presse Sports ; p. 237 : © Stanley Gontha/Presse Sports ; p. 243 : © Uwe Speck/WITTERS/Presse Sports ; p. 248 : © MacFarlane/Arsenal FC/Getty Images (h) ; © Getty Images ; p. 249 : © PA Images/Icon Sport ; p. 254 : © Landrain/Presse Sports ; p. 261 : © Nathan Ray Seebeck/Presse Sports ; p. 264 : © Action Press/Icon Sport ; p. 265 : © Bancet/Icon Sport ; p. 271 : © Biard/Icon Sport ; pp. 302-303 : © RONDEAU/Presse Sports.

Acknowledgments

Copyright Editions would like to thank all of the trademark holders (clubs, national associations, manufacturers, sponsors, etc.) for the visuals reproduced in this work.

Thank you as well to Thierry Freiberg, David Ausseil, and Charles-Henry Contamine for their help. The author would like to thank Patrick Battiston, Cyprien Cini (France, RTL), Bruno Constant (England), Garance Ferreaux (France, M6), Eric Frosio (Brazil), Stéphane Guy (France, Canal +), Franck Le Dorze (France, L'Equipe), Bixente Lizarazu, Roque Gaston Maspoli, Jean-Pierre Papin, Sergueï Polkhovski (Ukraine), Johnny Rep, Jean-Michel Rouet (France, L'Equipe), Alexis Menuge (Germany), Manuel Queiros (Portugal), Florent Torchut (Argentina), and Marie Yuuki (Japan).

Note to readers

In order to ensure a uniform appearance, all of the shirts have been redrawn in the most realistic manner possible. Where a particular shirt was worn during a season spanning two calendar years, the dates used in captions refer to the year in which the season finished (i.e. "2020" instead of "2019–2020"). The honours listed are correct as of the end of the 2024–2025 season. The international and continental honours only include the results achieved in the following competitions: FIFA World Cup, FIFA Confederations Cup, Copa América, Panamerican Championship, Olympic Games, UEFA European Football Championship, Gold Cup, Africa Cup of Nations, Asian Cup, FIFA Women's World Cup, UEFA Champions League (including the former European Cup), UEFA Europa League (including the former UEFA Cup and Inter-Cities Fairs Cup), UEFA Cup Winners' Cup, UEFA Super Cup, Intercontinental Cup, FIFA Club World Cup, Copa Libertadores, Supercopa Libertadores, Recopa Sudamericana, Copa Sudamericana, and Copa CONMEBOL.

The order in which national teams appear is based first and foremost on their performances at the World Cup, and then at other international tournaments. And the order in which clubs appear is based first and foremost on their performances in non-domestic tournaments.

In the event readers discover any errors, write to contact@copyright-editions.net so they can be corrected in future editions.

Standing in the third row: Paolo Rossi, Lothar Matthaüs, Igor Belanov, Oleg Blokhine, Karl-Heinz Rummenigge, Michel Platini, Hristo Stoitchkov, Florian Albert, Johan Cruyff, Denis Law, Bobby Charlton, Gianni Rivera, Josef Masopust.
Sitting in the second row: Allan Simonsen, Franz Beckenbauer, Luis Suarez, Alfredo Di Stéfano, Eusébio, Raymond Kopa.
Sitting in the front row: Jean-Pierre Papin, Zinédine Zidane, Ronaldinho, Luis Figo, Andrei Shevchenko.

2024
(home)

2024
(away)

2019
(home)

2016
(home)

2014
(away)

2013
(home)

2011
(away)

1998
(home)

1994
(home)

1986
(away)

1974
(home)

1962
(home)

1958
(home)

1958
(away)

1950
(home)

1949
(home)

1930
(home)

1919
(home)

The biggest stadium of all time

The Estádio Jornalista Mário Filho in Rio de Janeiro, Brazil, better known as the Maracanã, earned a place in the football record books during the final of the 1950 World Cup, when no fewer than 199,854 supporters packed into the stadium. The capacity of the Maracanã has since been reduced to 74,738 places for the final of the 2014 World Cup, Germany-Argentina (1-0 in extra time).

Reunited and multicultural

REUNITED AFTER THE FALL OF THE BERLIN WALL IN 1989, THE NATIONALMANNSCHAFT TOOK ADVANTAGE OF A NEW NATIONALITY LAW TO BECOME MORE MULTICULTURAL.

Although the German flag is black, red and yellow, the national team play in 19th century Prussian colours: white with black shorts. A national symbol since the 12th century, the eagle is a reference to the Holy Roman Empire. Separation came after World War II, and from 1949 to 1990 two different jerseys were worn by two different German teams: FRG (west) and GDR (east). In 1974, the World Cup came to West Germany and the two teams played each other in Hamburg. East Germany won 1–0. Although reunification (October 3, 1990) allowed Matthias Sammer, a future European Footballer of the Year winner (in 1996), to become the first East German to play for the Nationalmannschaft, the new Germany failed to perform at the very highest level. Euro 1996 and World Cup 2014 still remain the only tournaments won since reunification. All three other Germany's World Cups were won by those west of the great divide. Germany's 3–0 defeat by Croatia at the 1998 World Cup forced a complete rethink of the national set-up. The nationality law of January 1, 2000, which granted citizenship to all people born in the country, has allowed second-generation players such as Boateng, Khedira and Özil to emerge.

6
GLOBAL HONOURS
4 FIFA World Cups
1 Olympic Games (GDR)
1 Olympic Games (RDA)

3
CONTINENTAL HONOURS
3 UEFA European Football Championships

2014
World Cup–
winning jersey

13, lucky for some

BERLIN (GERMANY), OLYMPIASTADION
OCTOBER 16, 2012
Wearing 13 on his back, Thomas Müller was named Best Young Player at the 2010 World Cup in South Africa.

All players believe their little superstitions and habits give them an extra edge on the pitch. Few, for example, like to wear the number 13 shirt. In Christianity, Judas is synonymous with the number 13. The betrayer of Jesus was the 13th guest at the table of the Last Supper. And so it is strange that in Germany, with its two-thirds Christian population, wearers of the number 13 jersey have enjoyed great luck. In 1954, Max Morlock, wearing number 13, scored six goals in five matches at the World Cup in Switzerland. This included the goal that launched the comeback against Hungary in the 4th of July final. The Germans were down 2–0 and went on to win 3–2.

At the 1970 World Cup, Gerd Müller, also wearing 13, scored 10 goals in six matches. Four years later "Bomber 13" scored the winning goal in the final and gave the hosts a 2–1 victory over the Netherlands on July 7, 1974. The goal, his fourteenth and last in the World Cup, saw him overtake Frenchman Just Fontaine's record of 13 (all scored at the 1958 finals). The record stood until 2006 when the Brazilian Ronaldo bagged 15. In 2002, Michael Ballack, with 13 on his back, scored the only goal against the United States in the quarterfinals and against South Korea in the semifinals. Ballack was suspended for the final and Germany lost 2–0 against Brazil on June 30.

At the 2010 World Cup, the number 13 jersey was worn by 20-year-old Thomas Müller, who finished the tournament as joint top-scorer with five goals, and was also named its Best Young Player.

HAMBURG (GERMANY), VOLKSPARKSTADION
JUNE 22, 1974
West Germany skipper Franz Beckenbauer shakes hands with his East German counterpart Bernd Bransch before the only official match ever played between the two nations.

2025
(home)

2025
(away)

2024
(home)

2024
(away)

2022
(home)

2020
(home)

2018
(home)

2014
(home)

2012
(away)

1998
(home)

1994
(away)

1992
(home)

1990
(home)

1990
(away)

1984
(GDR - home)

1974
(FRG - home)

1974
(GDR - home)

1954
(FRG - home)

"Football is a simple game; 22 men chase a ball for 90 minutes and, at the end, the Germans win."

Gary Lineker

(England captain and 1986 World Cup Golden Boot winner, after losing the 1990 World Cup semifinal to Germany on penalties)

Gerd Müller is lifted in triumph after his winning goal against the Dutch in the World Cup final.

Green, white, and red = Blue

FOUR-TIME WORLD CUP WINNERS, ITALY ARE ONE OF THE FEW TEAMS NOT TO PLAY IN THE COLOURS OF THEIR NATIONAL FLAG.

Known by Italian fans as La Nazionale, the team was renamed La Squadra Azzurra ("the Blue Team") by French journalists during the World Cup in 1938, held in France. Originally, Italy played in white, one of the three colours of their national flag (along with green and red). Their first official international, on May 15, 1910, was played in white against France at the Milan Arena. Italy won 6–2. But just eight months later against Hungary on January 6, 1911, they put on a different colour shirt, a blue shirt. The colour, a seemingly strange pick, was chosen in honour of the Royal Family of the House of Savoy, whose official colour is blue. And Italy haven't looked back, becoming known as the Azzurri. All other Italian national teams followed suit, choosing blue as their colour. The white of old is used as a second strip, allowing Italians to remember their sporting origins.

5

GLOBAL HONOURS
4 FIFA World Cups
1 Olympic Games

2

CONTINENTAL HONOURS
2 UEFA European Football Championships

2006
World Cup–
winning jersey

BERLIN (GERMANY), OLYMPIASTADION
JULY 9, 2006

Italy captain Fabio Cannavaro hoists his nation's fourth World Cup after victory over France.

Donnarumma, number 1 at last

Gianluigi Donnarumma's number finally came up. The precocious Italian had been the undisputed number one goalkeeper for the Azzurri since 2018. But it took him several seasons to finally get the number on his back. He arrived in the shadow of Gianluigi Buffon, whom he replaced at halftime in a match against France during his first cap for Italy, on September 1, 2016 (1–3). For a good while, he had to make do with the numbers 12, 22, 20, and 21—with which he was crowned Champion of Europe at Wembley on July 11, 2021, after beating England (1–1, 4–3 on penalties). The number 1 had been passed to his senior colleague, Salvatore Sirigu.

None of this ever bothered him, though. He played his seven seasons at AC Milan wearing number 99, the year of his birth. At Paris Saint-Germain neither number 21 nor 99 were available. Spaniard Ander Herrera was already wearing number 21 when he arrived in the French capital in 2021, while article 576 of the regulations of the French Football League forbade the use of numbers above 30. Numbers 1, 16, and 30 were reserved for the sole use of goalies, but PSG already had four: Keylor Navas (1, a number he took from Buffon in 2019), Sergio Rico (16), Alexandre Letellier (30), and Denis Franchi (40). The Italian, therefore, obtained an exemption to be able to play with the number 50. At the start of the 2022–2023 season, this prohibition was struck from the regs and Donnarumma got his number 99 back. Navas left for Nottingham Forest on January 31, 2023, after which the number 1 definitively belonged to "Gigio," now free of all competition, including for Italy, where he got the captaincy in 2023.

**REGGIO EMILIA (ITALY),
MAPEI STADIUM-CITTA DEL TRICOLORE
JUNE 9, 2025**
Donnarumma holds off the Moldavia strikers during a qualification match for the 2026 World Cup (2–0).

2024
(home)

2022
(away)

2022
(home)

2021
(home)

2019
(third)

2016
(home)

2016
(away)

2014
(home)

2014
(away)

2010
(home)

1999
(away)

1994
(home)

1990
(away)

1982
(home)

1974
(away)

1948
(home)

1938
(away)

1910
(home)

Argentinian alphabet

UP UNTIL THE 1986 WORLD CUP, THE ARGENTINIAN FA WERE IN THE HABIT OF ASSIGNING NUMBERS BASED ON PLAYERS' SURNAMES. THE 10 WORN BY THE LEGENDARY MARADONA WAS AN EXCEPTION.

When dressing-room superstitions and wheeling and dealing are taken into account, allocating player numbers can be a headache for football authorities. The Argentinian Football Association (AFA) thought it had found a solution to the problem when, during the World Cups of 1974, 1978 and 1982, they distributed numbers in alphabetical order, using players' family names as a guide. Number 1, therefore, went to attacking midfielders Norberto Alonso in 1978 and Ossie Ardiles in 1982, and then to attacker Sergio Almirón in 1986. Goalkeeper Ubaldo Fillol received the 12, followed by the 5 and the 7. But there were some exceptions to this very Argentinian rule in 1982. Mario Kempes, number 13 in 1974, should have kept the 10 he wore when his country became world champions in 1978, which would have given Maradona the 12. But the national icon managed to keep hold of the 10, and Kempes wore 11 in the end. The system all but fell apart at Mexico 1986. Captain Daniel Passarella demanded the number 6 jersey that served him so well at club level, while Jorge Valdano wanted the 11. The AFA was eventually forced to give in to the players. It all worked out for the best, however, as the Albiceleste won the prestigious trophy for a second time that year.

8
GLOBAL HONOURS
3 FIFA World Cups
1 FIFA Confederations Cup
2 Olympic Games
2 CONMEBOL–UEFA Cup of Champions

16
CONTINENTAL HONOURS
16 Copas América

1986
World Cup–
winning jersey

From Maradona to Messi

Suddenly, the Argentinian supporters in Hamburg's World Cup Stadium turned away from their young number 10, Lionel Messi, who was doing his bit to beat a strong Ivory Coast side 2–1 in the opening Group C match of the 2006 finals (June 10). Their eyes were now fixed on another 10, "El Diez." And as the German cameras broadcast the arrival of the great Diego Armando Maradona onto the arena's giant screens, the crowd began long, appreciative chants: "Diego! Diego!"

The match became, in that moment, an afterthought. Until Messi, no player had truly managed to fill Maradona's shoes in the eyes of the Argentinian people, to the extent that on November 14, 2001, more than seven years after awarding him his 91st and final cap in a 2–1 win over Nigeria on June 25, 1994, the AFA decided to retire his number 10 jersey.

After reaching an agreement with the 2002 World Cup Local Organising Committee, the AFA drew up a list of 23 players, numbered 1 to 24. But FIFA rejected it. Article 26, Paragraph 4 of the governing body's regulations requires players to wear the numbers 1 to 23. FIFA President Sepp Blatter suggested giving the 10 to Roberto Bonano, the third-choice goalkeeper, but it was finally allotted to Ariel Ortega, who had already worn the famous number at France 1998. Subsequently, Pablo Aimar and Juan Riquelme took a turn, but it was the emergence of Messi, who made his debut in a friendly with Hungary on August 17, 2005, that would finally solve the "problem." Messi is the only player that Maradona, who inherited the number 10 jersey from the mighty Mario Kempes, sees as his rightful successor in the Argentinian national side.

MEXICO CITY (MEXICO), ESTADIO AZTECA
JUNE 22, 1986
Diego Maradona reaches above England goalkeeper Peter Shilton to punch home his famous "Hand of God" goal for Argentina in the quarterfinal of the World Cup.

After dribbling past 6 opponents and a 60-yard run, Maradona scores the "Goal of the Century."

"Maradona on the ball now. Two closing him down. Maradona rolls his foot over the ball

and breaks away down the right. He goes past a third, looks for Burruchaga.

Maradona forever! Genius! Genius! Genius! He's still going... Gooooal!

Sorry, I want to cry! Good God! Long live football!"

(Victor Hugo Morales's commentary—Radio Continental, Argentina).

2026
(home)

2024
(away)

2023
(home)

2022
(home)

2020
(away)

2019
(home)

2018
(away)

2016
(home)

2015
(away)

2014
(home)

2011
(away)

2006
(home)

2000
(home)

1997
(away)

1986
(home)

1982
(third)

1978
(home)

1930
(home)

Cock-a-doodle-not

IT MAY JUST BE A CURIOUS COINCIDENCE, BUT FRANCE SAW SOME OF ITS DARKEST DAYS WHEN THE ROOSTER ON ITS SHIRT WAS NOT FACING TOWARD THE HEART BUT RATHER AWAY FROM IT.

This might seem like an easily missed detail, yet the consequences have been dramatic. Immediately after their defeat in the 2006 World Cup final against Italy (1–1, then 3–5 on penalties), the rooster, the proud symbol of the French team since 1909, took a strange pirouette and switched direction to look outward (to the player's left). Wearing this new shirt, upon which the rooster turned its back on the heart, Les Bleus (the Blues) entered the darkest period in their history. In addition to their elimination from the group stages of UEFA Euro 2008 and the 2010 World Cup, France's image was tarnished by the players' revolt in South Africa, and Samir Nasri's insults directed at a journalist after France's elimination from the quarterfinals of Euro 2012 at the hands of Spain (0–2). It was as if the whole team had lost their heads. Things changed only when the rooster returned to its original position, following qualification for the 2014 World Cup. With their emblems looking them straight in the hearts again, Les Bleus were finalists on home soil in Euro 2016 (0–1 in extra time against Portugal), before winning a second World Cup in 2018.

2010
Jersey worn at World Cup with the rooster not facing toward the heart

FRANCE FFF

6
GLOBAL HONOURS
2 FIFA World Cups
2 FIFA Confederations Cups
1 Olympic Games
1 CONMEBOL–UEFA Cup of Champions

3
CONTINENTAL HONOURS
2 UEFA European Football Championships
1 UEFA Nations League

2018
World Cup–
winning jersey

Ten all the way

Rarely has a team's glory ever been so dependent on the number 10 as it has been with France. Yet Raymond Kopa does not feature at the top of the list of 112 players from 1945 to 2025 who have worn this number with Les Bleus. Kopa played just one club season wearing number 10—for Real Madrid (1956–1957)—and wore it only twice in forty-five caps. What's more, he played on right wing or as a second striker, although that didn't stop him being a real playmaker and team leader. As number 18 (then 9) of the France team, this earned him the 1958 Ballon d'Or following the national team's third place at the World Cup in Sweden.

With Michel Platini, and his heir Zinédine Zidane, there was no question of any other number. Both were Ballons d'Or. Platini gifted France its first major title (Euro 1984), while Zidane gave France its first World Cup star (1998). Their success reinforced the magic and the mystery of the number 10 in France, as well as a certain romantic idea of football. The same goes for their successors, despite them playing in different positions (as strikers). Karim Benzema played 68 of his 97 caps with number 10 on his shirt. Kylian Mbappé gave Les Bleus their second World Cup star in 2018 with the number 10 on his back in Benzema's absence, meaning that the latter had to make do with the number 19 when he returned to the squad. This was the number he wore when he started out at Lyon and the result of adding 10 + 9. You see, behind every great French player is the number 10, even if they don't wear it explicitly.

CLOCKWISE FROM TOP LEFT
Michel Platini (1976–1987), Zinédine Zidane (1994–2006), Karim Benzema (2007–2022), and Kylian Mbappé (2017–), have been bringing joy to the France team for fifty years.

MOSCOW (RUSSIA), LUZHNIKI STADIUM
JULY 15, 2018
Antoine Griezmann, Paul Pogba, and Kylian Mbappé (left to right)—all scorers in the World Cup final—show off the second star on their jerseys, following their victory over Croatia (4–2).

2024
(home)

2024
(away)

2022
(home)

2021
(home)

2016
(home)

2014
(away)

2013
(away)

2010
(home)

2009
(home)

2006
(away)

1998
(home)

1998
(away)

1984
(home)

1982
(home)

1978
(special)

1958
(home)

1909
(home)

1904
(home)

Four-star Celeste

TO URUGUAYAN EYES, THE PRESENCE OF FOUR STARS ON THE NATIONAL JERSEY SEEMS COMPLETELY NORMAL, DESPITE THE FACT THAT LA CELESTE HAS ONLY LIFTED TWO WORLD CUPS.

As is customary in football, each star symbolises a World Cup victory. This small South American nation, boasting a population of just 3.5 million, has two to its name (in 1930 and 1950). However, the reason that FIFA chose Uruguay as hosts for the first-ever World Cup in 1930 was due to their triumphs at consecutive Olympic Games, in 1924 and 1928, the only international football tournament in existence at the time. Uruguayans, therefore, regard this as akin to having won four World Cups. Copying Brazil, the first country to place stars on their jersey in 1970, they added four to their own in 2000. But FIFA amended their rules on April 1, 2010, stating that senior national teams should display a five-pointed star for each World Cup victory, "on the front of the shirt at chest level, immediately adjacent to the Official Member Association Emblem" (Article 16, Chapter 4: Playing Equipment). Uruguay circumvented this new ruling by inserting the stars within the emblem, without placing any outside. La Celeste will therefore remain a four-star team for the foreseeable future.

4
GLOBAL HONOURS
2 FIFA World Cups
2 Olympic Games

15
CONTINENTAL HONOURS
15 Copas América

2011
Copa América–
winning jersey

Cavani, faith in his 21

As much as Edinson Cavani worships Gabriel Batistuta, the Argentinian number 9, to the point of emulating his long, flowing hair, he is more a devotee of Zinédine Zidane in regards to his choice of jersey number. The Frenchman may have played the number 10 position (attacking midfield playmaker) on the pitch, but he wore number 7 on his back at FC Girondins de Bordeaux (1992–96), followed by number 21 at Juventus (1996–2001). Caviani (El Matador) has regularly worn the number 9 when playing at Paris SG in 2013, but he also wore the number 7 at US Palermo (2006–10) and at SCC Naples (2010–13). After starting out with the number 11, Cavani also wore the number 7 when he joined the national squad in 2008.

This choice was neither a happy coincidence nor the result of there being no other numbers available when Cavani began forging his professional career. It wasn't even a homage to Zidane. No, the reason is due to his deeply religious beliefs, since the number 7 in the Bible is synonymous with perfection. After all, six busy days of creation led to the plenitude of the seventh day. The number also evokes the Seven Sayings spoken by Jesus on the Cross, the Seven Trumpets of the Apocalypse, the seven Sacraments, the Seven Deadly Sins. . .

And although Cavani kept his number 7 at club level until his arrival in France, he soon abandoned it for the 21 when he joined the Uruguayan national side. This was a curious choice for a striker, but not for him. Ever fueled by his faith, this multiple of 7 evoked for him the number of quasi-divine protection. The number 21 is an indicator of chance, protection, success, and creative inspiration to rise higher in search of a certain plenitude. An expression of balance and harmony, 21 encourages success, dedication, and fulfillment. In short, 21 suited Cavani perfectly, until his retirement from the national team in 2022.

FORTALEZA (BRAZIL), ARENA CASTELÃO
JUNE 14, 2014, 24TH MINUTE
"This is crazy," Edinson Cavani seems to be saying, after scoring in his first World Cup match against Costa Rica (1–3).

2024
(home)

2024
(away)

2022
(home)

2022
(away)

2018
(home)

2013
(home)

2012
(away)

2010
(third)

2007
(home)

2006
(home)

2002
(home)

1999
(away)

1995
(home)

1994
(away)

1980
(home)

1950
(home)

1930
(home)

1907
(home)

United under the same colours

BEFORE BECOMING A MIGHTY WINNING MACHINA, SPAIN SUFFERED FOR MANY YEARS FROM THE RIVALRY BETWEEN THE CASTILIANS OF MADRID AND THE CATALANS OF BARCELONA.

Spanish football always produced great players, like Alfredo Di Stéfano, who was born in Argentina but played for Spain for most of his life, and won European Footballer of the Year in 1957 and 1959, and Luis Suárez, who won the same award in 1960. But for many years, La Roja (as the national team is known) was often relegated to a position of secondary importance in a country defined by regional differences. Undermined by the rivalry between Real Madrid, symbol of the establishment and centralised power, and Catalan representatives Barcelona, whose supporters were hostile to General Franco (1939–1975), the Spaniards rarely played and won together. That changed with the appointment of Madrid-born Luis Aragonés to the helm of the national side in 2004. Taking advantage of an exceptional generation of players led by Iniesta and Xavi, he was able to persuade the Madrid and Barcelona stars to unite with victory as their common goal. After winning Euro 2008, Aragonés made way for the former Real Madrid coach, Vicente Del Bosque, who built on the foundations laid by his predecessor to lead Spain to further glory at the 2010 World Cup and Euro 2012, the first time any nation won three consecutive major international competitions.

3
GLOBAL HONOURS
1 FIFA World Cup
2 Olympic Games

5
CONTINENTAL HONOURS
4 UEFA European Football Championships
1 UEFA Nations League

2012
European
Championship–
winning jersey

Rodri, golden 16

It's been a ritual set in stone for Rodrigo Hernández Cascante: to pull on a shirt displaying the name Rodrigo (even though all the commentators call him "Rodri"), then tuck it into his shorts, before stepping onto the pitch. Since 2016, his number has stayed the same, too, whether at clubs or for the national side: 16. The sole exception is from his 2018–2019 season at Atlético de Madrid, where he wore the number 14.

In numerology, the number 16 is often associated with the quest for self-knowledge and self-esteem. It is also synonymous with perseverance and spiritual awakening, but few of the great players have ever worn it. The Irishman Roy Keane and the Italian Daniele de Rossi are exceptions, as are the Argentinean Sergio "Kun" Agüero—the last player to have worn this number at Manchester City (2011–2015)—and Sergio Busquets. When Rodri took over the number 16 left vacant at the Citizens since Agüero left, it was indeed to pay homage to Busquets, eight years his senior, who also began his career as a defensive midfielder and of whom Rodri has always been a huge fan.

Manchester City gave Rodri his first victory in the Champions League, when he scored the winning goal of the 2023 final against Inter Milan (1–0). In the 2023–2024 season, the champion of England (with the Sky Blues) and Europe (with La Roja) only experienced one defeat—in the final of the FA Cup against Manchester United (1–2, on May 25, 2024)—compensated by the Ballon d'Or 2024. At twenty-eight, Rodri became the first player in the history of City to win it, and only the third Spaniard, after Alfredo Di Stéfano (1957 and 1959) and Luis Suarez (1960).

**VALLADOLID (SPAIN),
JOSE-ZORRILLA STADIUM**
NOVEMBER 19, 2023
Rodri led "La Roja" to victory over Georgia (3–1) in a qualification match for the Euros, which Spain would win eight months later after beating England in the final (2–1) in Berlin (Germany).

2024
(home)

2024
(away)

2022
(home)

2022
(away)

2018
(home)

2016
(away)

2013
(home)

2011
(home)

2010
(away)

2009
(home)

2008
(away)

1996
(home)

1996
(third)

1992
(home)

1990
(away)

1984
(home)

1964
(away)

1924
(home)

In the name of the rose

IN ADDITION TO THE THREE LIONS, TAKEN FROM THE COAT OF ARMS OF RICHARD THE LIONHEART, THE ENGLAND JERSEY FEATURES TEN TUDOR ROSES TO SYMBOLISE THE UNITY ACHIEVED IN THE 15TH CENTURY.

In the 43 years from 1966 to 2009, England changed their shirts 45 times. However, they have worn the coat of arms of Richard the Lionheart since their first match, on November 30, 1872, against Scotland (0–0). Reigning as king between 1189 and 1199, Richard I was the epitome of chivalry and royalty and his coat of arms took the form of three azure lions, one above the other. For the FA, the world's oldest football association (1863), "it was a powerful symbol raised by the throne of England during the Crusades and appropriated by a team heading into combat." To distinguish it from the crest of the cricket team, the FA added the floral emblem of England in 1949. This was a Tudor rose (red with a white centre), the symbol of the unification of the houses of Lancaster (red) and York (white) that occurred when the Tudor Henry VII married Elizabeth of York, putting an end to the War of the Roses (1455–1485). While the coat of arms used by the England rugby team has only one rose, the football version has ten, one for each league within the FA (in 1949), displayed on a field of silver.

1
GLOBAL HONOUR
1 FIFA World Cup

0
CONTINENTAL HONOUR

1966
World Cup–
winning jersey

A tradition dies hard

England likes to stay true to its traditions, including in football. The eleven players that begin a game wear the numbers 1 through 11. So when a regular starter like Rooney is selected as a substitute the number 10 he would normally wear is given to the player on the field. (*)

The first use of numbering in England dates back to August 25, 1928, when Arsenal and Chelsea both had numbers on their shirts when they played against The Wednesday (later renamed Sheffield Wednesday) and Swansea Town, respectively. The initiative did not continue. Following objections that adding numbers to the jerseys was not only too costly but unattractive, the league's governing body rejected a proposal requiring numbered shirts.

As for the England national team, they played with numbers for the first time in a competitive match on April 17, 1937, against Scotland. The numbers were assigned based on the players' positions: one for the goalkeeper, two for the right-back, and so on in ascending order up to the front, right to left, respecting the 2-3-5 formation, and ending with the number eleven, the left winger. The league finally followed suit on June 5, 1939. But with World War II beginning that year the change did not go into full effect until 1946.

The addition of players' names to jerseys happened much more recently. They first appeared on England shirts during Euro 1992 when UEFA made names mandatory. The Premier League then made names and assigning a number obligatory starting from the 1993–1994 season.

**ROME (ITALY),
STADIO OLIMPICO**
OCTOBER 11, 1997
The unforgettable image of Paul Ince's blood-soaked number 4 shirt during a qualifying match for the 1998 World Cup against Italy. FIFA now forces players to change their jerseys should they become bloodied.

(*) In some instances England cannot maintain this policy. Both FIFA and UEFA require players in the final stages of tournaments to keep their shirt number. But as can be seen in the qualifying games for the 2014 World Cup, England are assigning numbers on a match-by-match basis.

2024
(home)

2024
(away)

2022
(home)

2022
(away)

2020
(home)

2020
(away)

2016
(home)

2016
(away)

2012
(home)

2011
(home)

2010
(away)

2006
(home)

2002
(home)

1996
(away)

1985
(home)

1938
(home)

1930
(home)

1872
(home)

Mexico's nod to Aztec ancestors

DESPITE BEING DECIMATED BY SPANISH INVADERS, THE AZTECS ARE ALIVE AND WELL IN THE HEARTS OF MEXICANS, WHO HONOUR THEIR PREDECESSORS' FOUNDING MYTH ON THE NATIONAL FOOTBALL TEAM CREST.

Legend has it that the "Mexica" people, renamed "Aztecs" by the Spanish conquistadors, received an order from one of their gods, Huitzilopochtli, to abandon Aztlan and northern Mexico and settle wherever they found an eagle perched on a cactus, eating a serpent. Eight tribes marched for two hundred years, until one day the prophecy came true in the middle of the swamps. The travellers dried themselves off in 1325 and founded Tenochtitlan, which would eventually become the capital of a massive empire stretching from Texas to Honduras. The fall of Mexico on August 13, 1521 changed nothing. While large Spanish structures were built atop the spongy soil, the myth remained unshakeable for many Mexicans, to the extent that it figures on the national flag and on the jersey worn by El Tri, the nickname given to their team in reference to the country's three national colours: green (for hope), white (for purity) and red (for the blood of heroes). When saluting the flag, every player places his right hand by the coat of arms, palm facing down, hoping that a sprinkling of Aztec magic will provide an extra advantage in the 90-minute battle ahead.

2
GLOBAL HONOURS
1 FIFA Confederations Cup
1 Olympic Games

14
CONTINENTAL HONOURS
13 Gold Cups
1 CONCACAF Nations League

2006
Jersey worn
at World Cup

Campos, Mexico's colour man

When he was not keeping goal for his country, Jorge Campos was scoring goals for his clubs. While the actual figures vary from one Mexican statistician to another, what is clear is that he netted at least 35 in a 16-year career, 14 of those coming in just one season (1989–1990) for Mexican side Pumas. Before earning a reputation as a flying keeper, it was in the role of striker that he excelled while growing up in Acapulco, where he was born on October 15, 1966. But Campos' eccentric streak and taste for the spectacular did not end there. El Tri's legendary custodian also knew how to stand out from the crowd, appearing in some unique kits. During United States 1994, the first of his two World Cup experiences, he made a name for himself globally by wearing a fluorescent pink, green, yellow and red jersey/shorts get-up. The whimsical Mexican got into the habit of coming up with the creative jersey designs himself. His impressive total of 130 caps, amassed between 1991 and November 10, 2004, makes Campos not only one the most colourful goalkeepers of all time, but one of Mexico's best between the posts.

Jorge Campos in some of the eccentric, self-designed goalkeeping jerseys that became his trademark.

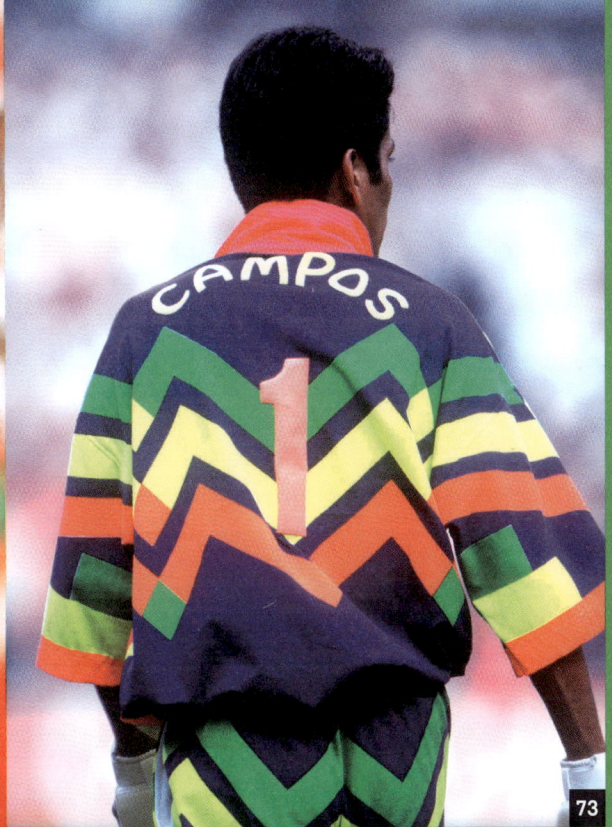

2026
(home)

2024
(home)

2024
(away)

2022
(home)

2021
(home)

2019
(home)

2018
(home)

2017
(home)

2015
(home)

2014
(home)

1998
(away)

1996
(home)

1994
(home)

1978
(away)

1978
(home)

1971
(away)

1970
(home)

1930
(home)

Soviet style

BEFORE GAINING A CERTAIN RETRO CACHET, THE HAMMER-AND-SICKLE-STAMPED JERSEY DRAPED THE BACKS OF THE SOVIET UNION'S BEST FOOTBALLERS AS THEY TOOK ON THE WORLD.

The iconic red top with "CCCP"—the Cyrillic alphabet's equivalent of "USSR" ("Union of Soviet Socialist Republics")—stamped across it was worn for the first time on August 21, 1923 in Stockholm in a match against Sweden. For a long time, the Soviets were content to test themselves exclusively in the Olympic Games (they won gold in 1956 and 1988), but only when they were not boycotting (as in 1948 in London and 1984 in Los Angeles). They finally made their World Cup debut in 1958. Although the sport was used as political propaganda, the USSR triumphed in just one non-Olympic international tournament, Euro 1960. They lost in the final of three others (the European Championships of 1964, 1972 and 1988). The USSR jersey would be given its final outing on November 13, 1991, in Larnaca, where its wearers defeated Cyprus 3–0. The break-up of the Soviet Union on December 26, 1991 led to the emergence of 15 separate national sides. Russia is considered by FIFA to be USSR's successor, and has inherited those now-defunct teams' results and records. It was a strange decision considering that a majority of the USSR's players came from the other 14 republics, such as Georgia and Ukraine.

2
GLOBAL HONOURS
2 Olympic Games

1
CONTINENTAL HONOUR
1 UEFA European Football Championship

1960
European Championship–winning jersey

Kiev, factory of champions

A dilapidated two-storey building—demolished to make room for a luxury hotel in 1998—at one time housed some of the gems of Soviet football. But those rising talents, surprisingly, did not belong to one of the powerful Moscow clubs. They were brought through the ranks in the utmost secrecy at Koncha-Zaspa, the training complex belonging to Dynamo Kiev that was founded in 1927 by the forerunners to the KGB. It was there, in a well-to-do suburb of Kiev, that Valeriy Lobanovskyi (1939–2002), known as "The Master," shaped the futures of many great players with an iron hand. Lev Yashin, the only goalkeeper to be named European Footballer of the Year (in 1963), is also the only Soviet winner of the prestigious award to not have been coached by the unsmiling Lobanovskyi. From 1973 to 1990, Lobanovskyi's team ruled over Soviet football, and even managed to transfer that success to the continental stage, defeating Hungarian side Ferencváros 3–0 to lift the European Cup Winners' Cup on May 14, 1975. They also won the same competition again in 1986. That time period saw Dynamo provide a majority of players to the USSR national team, with whom Lobanovskyi enjoyed three separate coaching spells. Two of his players captured the European Footballer of the Year award during his tenure at Dynamo, Oleg Blokhin (in 1975) and Igor Belanov (in 1986). After the fall of the Berlin Wall on November 9, 1989, he had a hand in the development of another future winner, Andrei Shevchenko, who received the accolade in 2004 while playing for AC Milan. The year before, Shevchenko laid his hands on the trophy that his mentor had always dreamed of holding: the Champions League.

**LEFT TO RIGHT (TOP),
AND LEFT TO RIGHT (BOTTOM)**
Lev Yashin (the only goalkeeper ever named European Footballer of the Year), Oleg Blokhin (second Soviet player to win the award in 1975), Igor Belanov (1986 European Footballer of the Year), and Andrei Shevchenko (2004's winner).

2024

(home)

2020

(away)

2018

(home)

2017

(home)

2016

(away)

2014

(home)

2014

(away)

2012

(home)

2010

(home)

2009
[home]

2004
[home]

1994
(USSR - home)

1990
(USSR - home)

1990
(USSR - away)

1988
(USSR - home)

1988
(USSR - away)

1966
(USSR - home)

1923
(USSR - home)

Big ideas, short sleeves

IN 2002 AND 2004, THE INDOMITABLE LIONS WERE AS UNPREDICTABLE WITH THEIR CHOICE OF SHIRTS AS THEY WERE ON THE PITCH. AND THEIR FASHION "FAUX PAS" ATTRACTED THE WRATH OF FIFA.

In 2000, keen to provide Adidas and Nike with competition, Puma produced several innovative football kits. For Italy, they created a set of tight-fitting jerseys designed to put an end to shirt-pulling. Then at the 2002 Africa Cup of Nations, they designed sleeveless shirts for Cameroon. FIFA, worried about the lack of space on the sleeves for their logo, banned the top from the World Cup. So Puma added black sleeves. And at the 2004 Africa Cup of Nations, Puma made the bold move of kitting Cameroon out with their UniQT jersey, a skin-tight, one-piece outfit. FIFA banned the team from wearing it in the quarterfinals, which Cameroon lost. On April 16, 2004, Cameroon were fined €128,900 and had six points deducted from their 2006 World Cup qualifying campaign, before FIFA had a change of heart the very next month and lifted the penalty. FIFA's Law 4, defining the players' equipment, had been found wanting. And it would not be the last time: on July 5, 2012, FIFA, under pressure from the Asian Football Confederation, authorised the wearing of a veil in women's tournaments.

1
GLOBAL HONOUR
1 Olympic Games

5
CONTINENTAL HONOURS
5 Africa Cups of Nations

2004
UniQt jersey, worn
during the Africa Cup
of Nations (skin-tight
one-piece outfit)

Milla: an African adventure

Roger Milla was not your average footballer. He was more of a dancer, in football boots. He proved as much at the 1990 World Cup, where Milla was ordered to play by the President of Cameroon. Seventeen minutes after replacing Maboang, the old Indomitable Lion roared in triumph by beating Silviu Lung in the Romanian goal. Milla ran to the corner flag, placed his left hand on his stomach, raised his right hand to the heavens and began to sway this way and that, inventing a dance that caught the attention of the watching world.

"I did it spontaneously. It wasn't planned out," he said. "It's not the Makossa, it's the Milla dance! It's a mix of all kinds of Cameroonian dances." Milla had launched a new craze and ever since then, footballers have tried to imitate him.

Milla headed for the corner flag to dance again after scoring once more in the 86th minute to complete a 2–1 victory. And he scored twice more against Colombia in the first knockout round (in the 106th and 109th minutes of extra time). Thanks to Milla's goals, an African team were in the quarterfinals for the first time (where they would lose 3–2 to England after extra time). Milla returned for the 1994 World Cup and one minute after replacing M'Fédé against Russia on June 28, the fans in San Francisco were on their feet. Milla showed off his dancing skills in front of 75,000 spectators, scoring his team's only goal in a 6–1 defeat. But Cameroon were out. The old lion retired having become the first African to play in three World Cups and the oldest player to play at and score in a World Cup (aged 42 years and 39 days).

NAPLES (ITALY), STADIO SAN PAOLO
JUNE 23, 1990
Roger Milla celebrates the first of his two goals against Colombia.

2025
(home)

2025
(away)

2024
(home)

2022
(home)

2022
(away)

2021
(home)

2018
(home)

2012
(away)

2012
(home)

2010
(away)

2002
(home)

2002
(home)

1998
(home)

1995
(home)

1990
(home)

1986
(home)

1984
(home)

1982
(home)

An ever-rising sun

MADE TO WAIT UNTIL 1988 TO MAKE THEIR FIRST APPEARANCE IN AN INTERNATIONAL TOURNAMENT, JAPAN IS NOW, ALONGSIDE SOUTH KOREA, THE MOST FORMIDABLE FOOTBALLING NATION IN ASIA.

In Japanese symbolism, the black crow, a figure of family love, is considered good luck. It heralded victory for the samurai and embodied their virtue. Thought to represent the sun, such as the one at the centre of the national flag, the bird's appearance in the empire's official records dates back to approximately 700 AD. The Japanese FA placed a three-legged crow at the heart of the team jersey's crest, its third foot clutching a red ball. But it took its time in bringing luck to the Land of the Rising Sun, as demonstrated by the results of their first two matches, 5–0 and 15–2 defeats to China and the Philippines respectively, on the 9th and 10th of May 1917. The "Samurai Blue" (a neutral colour, with no association to the red and white of the imperial flag) did not actually qualify for an international competition until the Asian Cup of 1988. The launch of the J. League on May 15, 1993 then precipitated the arrival of high-profile foreign players (Bebeto, Lineker, Schillaci and Stoichkov, among others) and managers (Ardiles, Littbarski, Wenger, and more). Reaching their first World Cup in 1998, Japan then qualified for the next five, reaching the quarter-finals in 2002, 2010 and 2018. First nation to win the Asia Cup four times, their players have well and truly established themselves at European clubs, and the women's team were crowned world champions in 2011, overcoming the United States on penalties.

0
GLOBAL HONOUR

4
CONTINENTAL HONOURS
4 Asian Cups

2011
Asian Cup–
winning jersey

Nakata: what's in a name?

The convoy of buses making their way to each match at Perugia's Renato Curi Stadium would often seem endless. Throughout 1999 alone, 30,000 football tourists made the long trip from Japan to profess their admiration for the new emperor, a man named Hidetoshi Nakata. The orange-haired midfielder was not, however, the first Japanese player to try his luck in Europe. But neither Yasuhiko Okudera, the first pioneer (in Germany, 1977–1986), nor Kazu Miura, the first to play in Italy (with Genoa in 1994), shared his head for business. Upon his arrival at Roma, Nakata pocketed $1 million simply by selling a limited series of 1,000 signed jerseys. As the owner of his own image rights via his Sunny Side Up management company, Nakata, who became interested in football after watching the long-running animated football programme Captain Tsubusa when he was a boy, also sold his image to a manga comic, a brand of saké, a video game and more. Perugia would not regret shelling out €2.4 million to Hiratsuka-based club Shonan Bellmare for Nakata in 1998. They sold the creative midfield man to Roma in 2000 for €21.7 million, and the Romans transferred him on to Parma for €28.4 million the following year. This sum is justified by the fact that Nakata, like David Beckham, was one of the first players to create a link between sport and fashion. In 2000, his name sold more jerseys than any other star save Ronaldo, and in 2004, he earned the same amount as the Brazilian (€16 million). Only Beckham (€30 million) and Zinédine Zidane (€19 million) were bringing in more at the time. He retired early on July 3, 2006, at just 29, in order to travel. But his business sense never left him. On March 30, 2011, a Taiwanese actress paid 27.6 million Yen to purchase a pair of Nakata's signed boots at auction.

**NANTES (FRANCE),
STADE DE LA BEAUJOIRE**
JUNE 20, 1998
Hidetoshi Nakata in action against Croatia in Japan's first World Cup, where they finished last in Group H.

2025
(home)

2025
(away)

2022
(home)

2021
(home)

2018
(home)

2017
(home)

2016
(home)

2012
(home)

2006
(away)

1998
(home)

1994
(away)

1994
(home)

1989
(home)

1983
(home)

1982
(home)

1970
(home)

1950
(home)

1930
(home)

At Christ's orders

THE IMPOSING COAT OF ARMS OVER THE PLAYERS' HEARTS SAYS MUCH ABOUT THE RICH PAST OF THIS LITTLE EUROPEAN COUNTRY AND THE FERVENT CATHOLIC FAITH OF ITS TEN MILLION INHABITANTS.

The coat of arms is placed over the heart and takes up a large space on the Portugal team's shirt. In itself, it sums up the history of Portugal. First of all, the cross pattée derives from the Military Order of Christ, a religious order that was involved in the founding of the kingdom of Portugal in the twelfth century and played a significant role in its extraordinary maritime expansion. (Indeed, this famous cross appeared on the white sails of the Portuguese caravels.) In the centre are five blue shields on a white background, from which comes the nickname Seleção das Quinas (Team of the Set of Five). They symbolise the victory over the five Moorish kings at the Battle of Ourique, on July 25, 1139, which enabled the proclamation of the first king of Portugal. The five white spots on each shield represent the five wounds of Christ on the Cross. The shields also appear on the Portuguese flag, from which derive the green and red used as colours for the national team's home kit. When playing away, the Seleção sometimes wears white and blue, the colours of the kingdom of Portugal, although it has on occasion played in black (2013) and in green (2016).

0
GLOBAL HONOUR

3
CONTINENTAL HONOURS
1 UEFA European Championship
2 UEFA Nations League

2016

European Championship–winning jersey

CR7th heaven

Cristiano Ronaldo looked set to experience a disastrous night on July 10, 2016. By the end it was one of the most beautiful moments of his life. As he was stretchered off the pitch in the twenty-fifth minute of the Euro 2016 final, it seemed as if his dreams of succeeding where the great Eusebio da Silva Ferreira had failed in the 1966 World Cup—when Portugal placed third—had vanished, and that his national team would not win their first trophy. But this would have been to underestimate such a true competitor. Returning to the bench with his thigh bandaged, he took on the role of a manager and supported his team from the sidelines. Once again, he found himself in the spotlight, even though he wasn't playing. Ronaldo's active presence on the bench helped to disconcert the French, who were defeated by a goal from Éder (Éderzito Lopes) in the 109th minute (1–0 in extra time). When Cristiano Ronaldo left the Stade de France, he felt as if he were in seventh heaven. "CR7" has become the eternal brand of an exceptional champion who drove his team to victory winning two Nations Leagues (in 2019 and 2025). A brand that, according to a 2017 estimate by the Portuguese Institute of Marketing Administration (IPAM), was worth $121 million (€102 million). And Ronaldo is keen to preserve and develop it. After starting his career at Sporting Lisbon in 2002 with number 28 on his back, number 7 soon became permanently glued to his initials. Except for when he moved to Real Madrid in 2009, where this number belonged to Raúl González Blanco. Upon the local star's departure for FC Schalke 04 one year later, Ronaldo dropped the 9 and took "his" 7 back.

Ronaldo has taken the CR7 name and made it famous in the most unlikely of arenas: the branding of his own line of underwear. He opened his first CR7 underwear store in Funchal, Portugal. Since then, the man with the perfect abs has extended his clothing line to include jeans, shoes, and accessories. On December 11, 2015, the new striker for Juventus FC (where Juan Cuadrado had been kindly asked to relinquish his number 7) partnered with the Portuguese Pestana Hotel Group to open six CR7 branded hotels by 2021.

SAINT-DENIS (FRANCE), STADE DE FRANCE
JULY 10, 2016
Cristiano Ronaldo, captain of Portugal, lifts the Henri Delaunay Trophy after beating France in the final of the UEFA European Championship (1–0 in extra time).

2025
(home)

2022
(away)

2022
(home)

2019
(home)

2014
(home)

2012
(home)

2012
(away)

2010
(home)

2006
(away)

1998

(home)

1998

(away)

1994

(home)

1992

(home)

1990

(home)

1984

(home)

1970

(home)

1966

(away)

1964

(home)

Not-so-Clockwork Orange

BIRTHPLACE OF "TOTAL FOOTBALL," THE NETHERLANDS HAVE APPEARED IN THREE WORLD CUP FINALS, LOSING EACH TIME.

The Netherlands have historically worn their iconic orange jersey, black shorts and orange socks with pride and panache. The black and orange harken back to the coat of arms of William of Orange, who achieved independence for the United Provinces. But one of the team's nicknames, "Clockwork Orange," stems more from the renowned "Total Football" they perfected than the colours on their backs. Over the years, however, things have not always gone like clockwork for the Flying Dutchmen. Although they secured their one and only European Championship title in 1988 (2–0 versus USSR, June 25), they were defeated in every one of the three World Cup finals they played in, including two in a row against the host nation in the 1970s (1–2 versus West Germany in 1974; 1–3 a.e.t. vs. Argentina in 1978; and 0–1 a.e.t. vs. Spain in 2010, in South Africa). Only Germany/West Germany have lost more often (four times), but they, at least, also have four triumphs to their name. Thirteen different teams have reached the World Cup final through the years, and the Oranje are one of just five of them to have never lifted the trophy, alongside Hungary, Czechoslovakia (two finals each), Croatia and Sweden (one appearance each).

0
GLOBAL HONOUR

1
CONTINENTAL HONOUR
1 UEFA European Football Championship

2010
World Cup–
runners-up jersey

Depay, designated survivor

Wesley Sneijder retired from international football on the evening of his 134th selection (a Dutch record) to the cheers of the crowd at the Johan-Cruyff ArenA, on September 6, 2018. As he stepped off the pitch in Amsterdam, in the sixty-second minute of a friendly match against Peru (2–1), he made one final, powerful gesture: "I symbolically hand over my jersey number [10] to [Memphis] Depay [scorer of the two winning goals]. He got my final Dutch jersey. He showed everyone how good he is at the moment. I hope he continues this way. We gonna enjoy him in the Dutch team." With this act, the man who came fourth in the 2010 Ballon d'Or passed on a message: at the age of twenty-four, it's time that Depay asserts his leadership over the new generation of Dutch players, and particularly those of Ajax Amsterdam, the surprise semifinalist of the Champions League a few months later (1–0, 2–3 against Tottenham, on April 30 and May 8, 2019, respectively).

Up until then, in both his club and international career, Depay had never worn the number 10, having preferred 22, 11, and above all the legendary number 7, which he wore at Manchester United for two seasons (2015–17), a time when the specialist online sports retailer Kitbag ranked Depay's shirt as 2015's third biggest seller, behind Lionel Messi and Cristiano Ronaldo. But ever since that September 2018 evening, he has worn number 10 for international games. "Since I joined the national team, [Wesley] took me under his wing. . . [He] was a big inspiration for me. [That he gave me his shirt and his number 10] is a wonderful compliment, so I'm glad to take it." Now it's up to him to prove himself worthy of this legacy.

HAMBURG (GERMANY), VOLKSPARKSTADION
SEPTEMBER 6, 2019
Ever since Wesley Sneijder's retirement from international football in 2018, Memphis Depay has worn number 10 for the Netherlands, as seen here when they beat Germany 4–2 in the qualifying stage for Euro 2020.

2024
(home)

2024
(away)

2022
(home)

2018
(home)

2013
(away)

2012
(home)

2008
(away)

1998
(home)

1996
(home)

1996
(away)

1988
(home)

1984
(home)

1978
(home)

1976
(away)

1974
(home)

1966
(home)

1934
(home)

1905
(home)

When the Vatreni inspired Barça

ON JUNE 3, 2019, THE WORLD CUP RUNNERS-UP WERE GREATLY SURPRISED TO DISCOVER THAT FC BARCELONA HAD RIPPED OFF THEIR FAMOUS CHECKERBOARD KIT, THE SYMBOL OF THIS YOUNG COUNTRY.

The Croatian international Ivan Rakitić has felt much less homesick at Barça since the 2019–20 season. Having featured vertical blue-and-garnet stripes on its kit for 120 years, Barça caused a stir in 2015, when it switched to horizontal stripes. But this was nothing compared to the surprise of June 3, 2019, when the club made a clean break with its traditional stripes by officially unveiling its new jersey. . . featuring a checkerboard design! Nike, Barça's kit supplier since 1998 (when Croatia finished third in the World Cup), justified this historic change by claiming it was a homage to the residential blocks laid out on a grid pattern so typical of the Catalan city. But the Vatreni (the Fiery Ones) didn't believe a word of it. Neither did the Croatian Football Federation (HNS). In a swiftly posted tweet, they cheekily referenced Barça's rip-off of the young country's emblematic checkerboard shirt: "Nice try @FCBarcelona, but you can't beat red-and-white checkers." and followed up with "Well, we are convinced that @ivanrakitic will surely enjoy the new @FCBarcelona kit!"

2020
FC Barcelona home jersey

0 GLOBAL HONOUR

0 CONTINENTAL HONOUR

2018
World Cup–
runners-up jersey

Modrić, from 14 to number 1

On December 3, 2018, Luka Modrić stepped forward onto the balcony of the Grand Palais in Paris as number one. In the absence of Cristiano Ronaldo and Lionel Messi—winners of the last ten Ballon d'Or (five each)—not to mention Neymar, who skipped the ceremony in favor of playing *Call of Duty* with his compatriots Marquinhos and Thiago Silva, the captain of Croatia saw his immense talent finally rewarded. Winner of the UEFA Champions League with Real Madrid six months earlier (3–1 against Liverpool), and finalist of a World Cup in which he was voted best player, Modrić lifted the sixty-third Ballon d'Or.

Aged thirty-four, Modrić joins his idol Johan Cruyff (triple winner: 1971, 1973, and 1974) in this footballers' pantheon. Indeed, when he began his international career in 2006, Modrić wore the number 14 shirt in homage to "the Flying Dutchman," and he kept it for the next three years. Later, at Tottenham Hotspur, he refused to wear the prestigious number 10, despite being the perfect playmaker. No, Modrić would keep number 14 throughout his four years in the Premier League.

But when Modrić arrived at Real, in 2012, he could no longer allow himself to keep the number of Cruyff, who had played such a key role at Barça, the Madrid club's historic rival. So Modrić fell back on number 19 for five years. When the Colombian player James Rodriguez left for Bayern Munich in 2017, the number 10 became free, and Modrić naturally took it. Yet switching from 14 to 10 changed nothing about his extraordinary technique and tactical vision, which enabled him to become the first player of the former Yugoslavia, and the first Croatian, to receive the Ballon d'Or (Davor Šuker had finished second, behind Zinedine Zidane, in 1998). Modrić is quite simply the top footballer on the planet.

MOSCOW (RUSSIA), LUZHNIKI STADIUM
JULY 15, 2018
Luka Modrić, Croatia's captain and number 10 during the 2018 World Cup final (2-4 against France).

2024
(home)

2022
(away)

2022
(home)

2020
(home)

2018
(away)

2016
(home)

2016
(away)

2014
(home)

2012
(home)

2012
(away)

2006
(home)

2006
(away)

2004
(home)

1998
(home)

1998
(away)

1996
(home)

1994
(home)

1990
(home)

Football's first ladies

IN THE UNITED STATES, THE WOMEN'S NATIONAL TEAM HAS ACHIEVED A LEVEL OF POPULARITY AND NOTORIETY RARELY SEEN IN OTHER COUNTRIES.

After the collapse of the NASL, soccer appeared to have had its day in the United States. But the success of women's soccer and the start of a new men's professional league—Major League Soccer—in 1996 helped the sport survive and grow. Now, almost 30 years after the end of the NASL, soccer is thriving and has become an important part of the sporting landscape in the US. Six years after the US Women played their first match on August 18, 1985), the team triumphed in the inaugural 1991 Women's World Cup in China. It wasn't until the ninth edition, in 2023, that the Americans stopped finishing on the podium. But they remain the only team to wear four stars on their jerseys (1991, 1999, 2015, 2019) and to have won five of the first eight gold medals at the Olympics. The success of the 1994 Men's World Cup helped launch MLS, and the league has grown to include 19 teams. The fan support has steadily improved over the years and MLS is now ranked seventh in attendance for all leagues around the world. Although the American women have had the misfortune of witnessing two professional leagues fold, a third, which is being run by the US Soccer Federation and called the National Women's Soccer League (NWSL), began in the spring of 2013. With a new business model and the main goal of sustainability, the league's aim is to help the women's game develop even more in the US. The hope is that Team United States will remain on top of the world. Their championship, launched in 2001, has fourteen franchises. Two more will be created in Massachusetts (Boston Legacy) and Colorado (Denver Summit FC), in 2026.

9
GLOBAL HONOURS
4 FIFA Women's World Cups
5 Olympic Games

9
CONTINENTAL HONOURS
9 Gold Cups

2019
World Cup–
winning jersey

Women and the beautiful game

Women have played football for almost as long as men, and the women's game has attracted audiences that rival the men's. Indeed, in England, the popularity of women's football in the early 20th century was so great that some say it jeopardized its own future.

One game in particular was pivotal in the history of the women's game. On December 26, 1920, 53,000 fans attended a match at Goodison Park (home to Everton F.C.) featuring Dick, Kerr's Ladies F.C., named after a munitions factory where women worked during World War I. Records indicate that even more fans tried to see the game but were turned away. Within one year women's teams were banned from all FA affiliated grounds. Some players and press have speculated that the decision was made in an effort to keep audiences focused on the men's game.

The ban wasn't lifted until 1969, the same year that the famed Doncaster Belles were founded by lottery ticket sellers at Belle Vue stadium, the home of Doncaster Rovers F.C. The Belles went on to dominate the sport in England winning six FA Women's Cups and reaching the final on a further seven occasions. Women's football was embraced in other countries, notably within Scandinavia and the US, especially during the second half of the 20th century. Colleges and universities fostered the sport and it flourished in the 1980s with the celebrated North Carolina university team who won 21 of the first 31 women's National Collegiate Athletics Association (NCAA) titles.

One of the iconic images of the 1990s is of the US defender Brandi Chastain jubilant after scoring the decisive penalty against China in the final of the 1999 World Cup (0–0, 5–4 on penalties, July 10). She graced the covers of numerous prestigious publications such as Time, Newsweek and Sports Illustrated propelling the women's game into the limelight once more.

LEFT TO RIGHT (TOP), AND LEFT TO RIGHT (BOTTOM)
North Carolina forward Mia Hamm at Fetzer Field, Chapel Hill, North Carolina (1993); Leonie Maier of Germany (2nd in FIFA's world rankings behind the US) and Shinobu Ohno of Japan (ranked 3rd) during an international friendly at the Allianz Arena in Munich, Germany (June 29, 2013); US defender Brandi Chastain on the cover of Sports Illustrated (July, 1999); Megan Rapinoe proudly displays the trophy following the United States's fourth world cup title, in 2019.

Why Brandi Chastain and the U.S. Women's
Soccer Team Were Unbeatable

2025
(home)

2025
(away)

2024
(home)

2023
(home)

2022
(home)

2022
(away)

2021
(away)

2015
(home)

2015
(away)

2014
(home)

2012
(home)

2011
(home)

2007
(away)

1999
(home)

1996
(home)

1995
(home)

1991
(home)

1995
(home)

Regal roots

NAMED "CLUB OF THE CENTURY" BY FIFA IN 2000, REAL MADRID, OFFICIALLY FOUNDED ON MARCH 6, 1902, DID NOT ORIGINALLY PLAY IN THE NOW FAMOUS ALL-WHITE STRIP.

A blue diagonal stripe, like the one on their crest, appeared across the Spanish club's jerseys in the early days. Captivated by the elegance of London-based side Corinthians, who played in white shirts and trousers, the Real management decided to change to all white. After becoming known as Los Merengues, they added buttons as well as the club crest (which remains there to this day) at chest level. The "White House" received royal patronage and became "Real Madrid Club de Fútbol" in 1920, and the crown of Alphonso XIII was added to the top of their crest. It was replaced in 1931 by a blue band representing the region of Castile, upon the establishment of the Second Republic. Madrid regained its "Real Corona" (royal crown) in 1941, two years after the end of the Spanish Civil War. So as to avoid offending the United Arab Emirates, with whom they agreed to open an island theme park in 2015, the club removed the Catholic cross from the crown in their crest in 2012.

32
GLOBAL HONOURS
15 UEFA Champions Leagues
2 UEFA Europa Leagues
6 UEFA Super Cup
9 Intercontinental Cups

70
NATIONAL HONOURS
36 Spanish Leagues
20 Spanish Cups
13 Spanish Super Cups
1 Copa de la Liga

2014
Spanish League–
winning jersey

Mbappé, stronger than CR9

The "royal wedding" between Kylian Mbappé and Real Madrid on July 16, 2024 drew huge crowds. More than 500,000 locals requested to attend the official ceremony at the Santiago-Bernabeu stadium. A record! The online ticketing system crashed several times. This frenzy around the arrival of the 2018 World Cup winner was reflected in the official merchandise stores on July 11, when the shirt bearing Mbappé's name above the number 9 sold out in a flash. Fans had to dig deep though, with the basic version costing €120, and the premium one (as worn by the players) selling for €170, plus an extra €15 each for the Champions League badge. This didn't discourage the afficionados, who were prepared to wait eight weeks for their orders on the Real webstore to be fulfilled. "Mbappé-mania" seems to have exceeded even the "CR9-mania" that accompanied the arrival of Cristiano Ronaldo, who also began his romance with Madrid wearing the number 9 in 2009. According to the Portuguese sports daily A Bola, "CR9" sold 3,300 units a day during his first season, for a total of over a million shirts—an achievement that David Beckham managed in just six months in 2003—at a price of €80 (the equivalent of €107 in 2025). Mbappé's shirt, however, was shifting around 7,000 a day before he'd even played his first official match with Real, let alone finished the season with the nickname "Pichichi" and the honour of being top scorer in the Liga (thirty-one goals in thirty-four matches).

TOP TO BOTTOM
Since 2024, Kylian Mbappé has followed in the footsteps of Cristiano Ronaldo, the top scorer in the history of Real Madrid (450 goals in 438 matches, between 2009 and 2018).

2026
(home)

2026
(third)

2023
(home)

2023
(away)

2022
(home)

2021
(away)

2018
(home)

2015
(away)

2012
(home)

2004
(home)

2000
(away)

1998
(home)

1989
(home)

1986
(away)

1984
(home)

1956
(home)

1940
(away)

1916
(home)

Barça: more than a club

FORMED IN 1899, FC BARCELONA EMBODIES A DEEP-ROOTED CATALAN IDENTITY IN SPAIN, UNLIKE THEIR ETERNAL RIVALS FROM THE CAPITAL, REAL MADRID.

The eleven men—six Catalans, two Englishmen, two Swiss and a German—who responded to an advertisement in Los Deportes on October 22, 1899 had no way of realising that they were in the process of founding what would become one of the most powerful clubs in the world. The blaugrana colours (blue and dark red) were adopted the same year, ahead of a match against Català. And while their crest, shaped like a bowl from 1910 onwards, was the subject of various minor amendments up to 2002, it still takes its inspiration from the coat of arms of the city of Barcelona, which features the St. George's Cross alongside the Catalan flag.

Barça has always conveyed a strong Catalan identity, opposing the centralism of Madrid, to the extent that the club was closed for six months after the Spanish national anthem (Marcha Real) was booed and whistled at on June 14, 1925. On August 6, 1936, a month after the start of the Spanish Civil War, then club president Josep Suñol, a Republican and Catalan nationalist, was arrested by forces loyal to General Franco and shot on the spot. Today, Barcelona remains a club that is anchored in its traditions yet still exudes a fearsome modernity.

20

GLOBAL HONOURS
5 UEFA Champions Leagues
3 UEFA Fairs Cups
4 UEFA Cup Winners' Cups
5 UEFA Super Cups
3 FIFA Club World Cups

77

NATIONAL HONOURS
28 Spanish Leagues
32 Spanish Cups
15 Spanish Super Cups
2 Copas de la Liga

2015
Champions League–
winning jersey

Lamine Yamal, the heir

Lamine Yamal may have got used to adding extra zeroes to his contracts, but he was happy to agree to put only one on the back of his shirt. That too was new. Aged seventeen, the right winger had already picked up quite a few numbers, but none containing a zero: there was number 41, during his first professional season in 2023; numbers 27 and 19 with Barça; and numbers 15, 17, and 19 with La Roja. Indeed, it was with number 19 on his back that he became a European champion after beating England 2–1 in the final of Euro 2024. Yamal's father was a huge fan of Lionel Messi, who had worn number 19 when he started at Barça in 2004. And so his son adopted it for the 2024–2025 season. But Yamal had his eyes on another set of digits worn by "La Pulga": number 10. At the time, it belonged to Ansu Fati, over on the left wing— another Catalan prodigy whose career has been plagued by injuries.

Yamal was used to changing numbers each season, but he decided to emulate Messi by definitively adopting the number 10 (starting from the 2025–2026 season), as well as extending his contract with the Catalonian club by five years. This means that he'll stay at the club that trained him until June 30, 2031, when he will still only be twenty-three. And just like Gavi and Pau Cubarsi, his buyout fee will jump to a billion euros and his earnings will reach €15 to €20 million net per year depending on bonuses (goals scored, decisive passes, Ballon d'Or).

Since the start of the 2025–2026 season, Yamal has worn the number 10 for the national team, too, for greater visibility and clarity. Here's hoping he can achieve with it what one of his predecessors, Cesc Fabregas, did: the historic hat-trick of Euro 2008–World Cup 2010–Euro 2012.

KOBE (JAPAN), NOEVIR STADIUM
JULY 27, 2025
The first time Lamine Yamal wore his new shirt with the number 10 was for a friendly match against Vissel Kobe (3–1) during Barça's tour of Japan.

2026
(home)

2025
(third)

2025
(home)

2021
(home)

2020
(home)

2017
(home)

2014
(away)

2013
(home)

2010
(home)

2009
(home)

2000
(home)

1992
(away)

1984
(home)

1984
(away)

1979
(home)

1977
(away)

1929
(home)

1899
(home)

"La mitad màs uno"[(*)]

(*)Half plus one

FOUNDED BY FACTORY WORKERS, LOS BOSTEROS ("THE BUMPKINS") STATE PROUDLY THAT THEY ARE SUPPORTED BY OVER HALF OF ALL FOOTBALL FANS IN ARGENTINA.

The Genoese immigrants who established the Buenos Aires club on April 3, 1905 kept things simple—they gave it the name of the port district, "La Boca," and added the word "Juniors" as a tribute to football's British roots. Realising that none of the colours they chose (pink, sky blue, or Juventus-style black and white stripes) were suitable, one of them suggested two years later that the club adopt the colours of the next boat that sailed into port. That boat happened to be Swedish, and Boca Juniors' now revered blue and yellow (originally a diagonal yellow stripe, but changed to a horizontal one in 1913) was born. When Mauricio Macri added two white stripes above and below the yellow band upon becoming club president in 1996, Diego Maradona himself threatened to stop wearing the jersey, before later changing his mind. Coca-Cola was forced to follow suit when Los Xeneizes ("the Genoese") asked the company to change the colour of the world-famous logo if it wanted to succeed Pepsi as jersey sponsor in 2004. The reason? Red and white are the colours of River Plate, the club's eternal rivals. Boca's stadium, known as "La Bombonera," thereby became the only place in the world where Coca-Cola's logo is black and white.

18
GLOBAL HONOURS
6 Copas Libertadores
1 Supercopa Libertadores
4 Recopas Sudamericana
2 Copas Sudamericana
1 Copa de Oro
1 Copa Master de Supercopa
3 FIFA Club World Cups

43
NATIONAL HONOURS
35 Argentinian Leagues
4 Argentinian Cups
2 Copa de la Liga Profesional
2 Supercopas Argentina

2003

Argentinian League–,
Copa Liberatores–,
and Intercontinental
Cup–winning jersey

Riquelme, heir of discord

A former Boca star (1981–1982 and 1995–1997), Diego Maradona continued to support the club closest to his heart from the balcony of his private box.

Juan Román Riquelme could not have dreamt of a greater public tribute than the one he received on November 10, 2001, the day Diego Maradona retired from the game. After the gala match held in his honour at La Bombonera, El Pibe de Oro ("the gilded kid") took off his Argentina shirt to reveal the Boca Juniors one, printed with the number 10 and the name of his successor: Riquelme. Having worked his way up through Argentinos Juniors (just as his idol had), Riquelme had already come on for Maradona after halftime of his last official match, a Superclásico away win over River Plate (2–1) on October 26, 1997.

Riquelme proudly wore the number 10 for six months, before leaving for Barça in his idol's footsteps. But it was at Villarreal (2003–2007) that Riquelme rose to prominence. Yet despite earning 51 caps and scoring seventeen goals for Argentina between 1997 and 2008, he never managed to truly fill Maradona's shoes, even going as far as to quit international football after the 2006 World Cup. Alfio Basile, the new Argentine coach, persuaded Riquelme to return to beat Chile (2–0) on October 13, 2007, but Riquelme definitively shut the door on La Albiceleste in March 2009, enraged after being ignored by Basile's successor—none other than Maradona! "Riquelme is too slow," claimed Maradona, who, from when he took over as coach in October 2008 until he left after the 2010 World Cup, never picked the skilled midfielder. "El Ultimo Numero Diez" (the last number ten), as Riquelme was known, and who had a statue at La Bombonera erected in his honour, did gain some semblance of revenge on "El Diez": in 2008, Riquelme was named "Most Popular Player in Boca's History" by fans, receiving 33.37% of the vote compared to Maradona's 26.42%; and on December 18, 2023, Riquelme was elected president of the club, winning 65% of the more than 43,000 votes counted, a record in the history of Argentine football.

Juan Riquelme, seen here battling with River Plate captain Marcelo Gallardo, was named "Most Popular Player in Boca's History" by the club's fans in 2008.

2026
(home)

2026
(away)

2025
(home)

2021
(home)

2021
(away)

2018
(home)

2017
(home)

2016
(away)

2012
(home)

2006
(home)

1997
(home)

1992
(home)

1986
(home)

1955
(away)

1931
(home)

1919
(home)

1908
(home)

1905
(home)

"Il club più titolato al mondo"[(*)]

(*)The most successful club in the world

21 YEARS AFTER SAVING AC MILAN FROM BANKRUPTCY, SILVIO BERLUSCONI SAW HIS GRAND DREAMS COME TRUE IN 2007 AS THE CLUB BECAME THE MOST TROPHY-RICH TEAM IN THE WORLD.

"Il club più titolato al mondo." Following the FIFA Club World Cup final on December 16, 2007, those six words were embroidered in gold on AC Milan's jersey, under the crest. This 18th international title propelled the club above Boca Juniors, the Argentinians they just defeated 4–2, meaning Milan now had the most continental and global trophies among all the teams of the world. In addition, it represented the realisation of a long-held dream for Silvio Berlusconi, who had bought the then financially troubled outfit on February 20, 1986. It was a curious fate for a football and cricket (up to 1905) club founded on December 16, 1899 by ten Englishmen and seven Italians whose first president, Herbert Kilpin, was a British vice-consul. Following the English trend at the time, the red and black striped jersey was adopted from the outset. Red for the devil and black to instill fear. They have not always been fearsome, and even less so since 2014 and the new world domination of Real, now the most successful club on the planet, with 26 titles.

18
GLOBAL HONOURS
7 UEFA Champions Leagues
2 UEFA Cup Winners' Cups
5 UEFA Super Cups
4 FIFA Club World Cup

32
NATIONAL HONOURS
19 Italian Leagues
5 Italian Cups
8 Italian Super Cups

1990
UEFA Super Cup–
winning jersey

The Maldinis: what a dynasty

In the Maldini family, football is passed down from father to son. As is AC Milan. Cesare, a centre-back from 1954 to 1966, gifted the club its first Champions League, in 1963. His son Paolo, also a defender, gave them five more. In fact, Paolo played his entire career at the club, winning twenty-six trophies with them and setting a record for the most matches played for the Rossoneri (902). When he hung up his studs in 2009, the club retired his number 3 shirt in appreciation of his loyalty.

Grandson Christian, born in 1996, also cut his teeth at the club, but he didn't make it past juniors, plying his trade as a centre-back in the lower leagues. However, his younger brother Daniel (b. 2001) has forged a glittering career with the senior team, including a scudetto in 2022. And although he holds Venezuelan nationality through his mother, Adriana, Daniel has also worn the Italy shirt. His first cap was on October 14, 2024 against Israel (4–1). What's more, he plays as an attacking midfielder—and sometimes a striker—without an attributed shirt number, unlike grandpa Cesare who wore the number 5 throughout most of his career.

It's not unusual to see one or more sons follow in their father's footballing footsteps: Erling and Alf-Inge Haaland (Norway); Youri and Jean Djorkaëff (France); Marcus and Kephren after their father Lilian Thuram (France); Michael and Brian after Finn Laudrup (Denmark). But three generations of footballers playing at such a level remains a rarity. Michael Laudrup's two sons, Mads and Andreas, are also professional, but neither has been capped for their country.

CLOCKWISE FROM TOP LEFT
Cesare Maldini lifts AC Milan's first-ever Champions League trophy; his son Paolo also became an emblematic captain for the team; grandson Daniel is the third to wear the Rossonero shirt.

2026
(home)

2026
(away)

2024
(home)

2024
(away)

2023
(home)

2022
(home)

2021
(home)

2021
(away)

2020
(home)

2016
(away)

2013
(home)

2007
(away)

2003
(home)

2000
(home)

1998
(third)

1982
(home)

1969
(home)

1963
(away)

MILAN (ITALY), SAN SIRO STADIUM
JANUARY 15, 2012
Zlatan Ibrahimović soars into the air to control the ball, watched by the Maicon, during the "Derby della Madonnina" against Inter Milan (0–1).

Los Millonarios back from the brink

IN 2011, THE UNTHINKABLE HAPPENED TO CLUB ATLÉTICO RIVER PLATE. THE OUTFIT, FOUNDED ON MAY 25, 1901 AND BECOMES DRAWS ITS SUPPORT FROM TRADITIONALLY MIDDLE-CLASS AREAS OF BUENOS AIRES, WAS RELEGATED FOR THE FIRST TIME IN ITS IMPRESSIVE HISTORY.

La Màquina ("The Locomotive"), a nickname given to River Plate in the 1940s when the team was running away with the Argentinian League, derailed badly on June 26, 2011. For the first time since May 2, 1909, the date of its top-flight debut, River Plate was demoted following an aggregate play-off defeat at the hands of Belgrano (0–2, 1–1). The return leg did not even last the full 90 minutes, as the club's fans invaded the Estadio Monumental pitch towards the end. Aside from the significant damage caused to the stadium, 89 people were injured and another 50 or so were arrested. Once tensions subsided, River Plate fans eventually proved their love for the team's iconic jersey, white with a red diagonal stripe (added by the club's Genoese founders during the Buenos Aires carnival of 1905 for a splash of colour). Supporters turned out in huge numbers to support Los Millonarios in the second division, and they had their loyalty rewarded on June 23, 2012, when River returned to the top tier of Argentinian football by beating Almirante Brown 2–0, courtesy of a brace from French striker David Trezeguet.

18
GLOBAL HONOURS
4 Copas Libertadores
1 Copa Sudamericana
3 Recopas Sudamericana
1 Supercopa Libertadores
1 Copa Interamericana
1 FIFA Club World Cup
6 Copa Aldao / 1 Copa Levain

45
NATIONAL HONOURS
38 Argentinian Leagues
3 Argentinian Cups
4 Supercopas Argentina

1986
Copa Liberatores–
winning jersey

The chicken and the lion

It sounds like a story borrowed from Aesop's Fables. The men that ran River Plate, known as Los Millonarios, were fed up with being referred to as Las Gallinas ("The Chickens"), ever since their unexpected 4–2 defeat by Uruguayan giants Peñarol in the final of the 1966 Copa Libertadores. During their next league match, Club Atlético Banfield supporters released a hen wearing a red ribbon onto the pitch, and the derogatory nickname stuck. In 1986 then club president Hugo Santilli (1983–1989) decided to address the issue by adding the emblem of a lion drawn by Caloi, a famous Argentinian caricaturist, to the chest of the jersey. He also removed the red stripe from the back of the shirt. This change in particular caused uproar among River's supporters, furious that their jersey now looked the same as everyone else's from behind. Curiously, it was while wearing this new-look top that River enjoyed the most successful period in their history, claiming a 13th Argentinian Championship, a maiden Copa Libertadores, a first and only Intercontinental Cup and a Copa Interamericana, all in the space of just two years. Taking over from Santilli, Alfredo Davicce, who ran the club from 1989 to 1997, removed the lion and restored the stripe. And River Plate would have to wait ten years before winning another international trophy. The moral of the tale? Better to be lionhearted than a chicken.

BUENOS AIRES (ARGENTINA), ESTADIO MONUMENTAL
JUNE 23, 2012
Thanks to a brace from French ace David Trezeguet against Almirante Brown, River Plate make an immediate return to the Argentinian Primera División a year after being relegated for the first time.

2026
(home)

2025
(away)

2024
(away)

2013
(away)

2005
(home)

2004
(third)

2004
(away)

1997
(home)

1995
(home)

1995
(away)

1984
(home)

1984
(away)

1982
(away)

1965
(away)

1964
(away)

1932
(home)

1920
(home)

1903
(home)

From the gym to FC Hollywood

CREATED AFTER SPLITTING FROM A MULTI-SPORT ORGANISATION, BAYERN MUNICH HAVE BECOME, IN SPITE OF NUMEROUS INTERNAL PROBLEMS, ONE OF THE MOST WELL-SUPPORTED AND POWERFUL CLUBS IN EUROPE.

On the morning of February 27, 1900, the Munich gymnastics club of MTV 1879 refused to allow its football section to join the German FA (DFB). That very evening, 11 of its members founded FC Bayern Munich ("Bayern" being the German word for "Bavarian"). However, the rise to power of the Nazis in 1933 brought their gradual development to an abrupt halt. Their president and coach, both Jewish, were forced to flee Germany, while Bayern, now referred to as the "Jewish club," battled against ignorance at home. It took them until 1965 to obtain promotion to the Bundesliga, two years after the launch of the professional championship. Despite several high-profile dramas that led to them gaining the nickname "FC Hollywood," the Bavarians have since become one of the most respected, stable and formidable clubs in Europe. Bayern's jersey boasts five stars. In order to thank and honour the team's iconic performers of the past, a Bayern "Hall of Fame" was created, featuring 14 Germans as well as Brazilian forward Giovane Elber and French defender Bixente Lizarazu.

14 GLOBAL HONOURS

6 UEFA Champions Leagues
1 UEFA Europa League
1 UEFA Cup Winners' Cup
2 UEFA Super Cup
4 FIFA Club World Cup

70 NATIONAL HONOURS

34 German Leagues
20 German Cups
6 German League Cups
10 German Super Cups

2013
German League–
winning jersey

Harry Kane is no longer cursed

When he received a yellow card that resulted in his suspension for Bayern Munich's decisive clash with Leipzig in the Bundesliga, Harry Kane must have thought his "curse" would follow him to the end of his career. It didn't get any better when he came down from the stands of the Red Bull Arena to celebrate Bayern Munich's victory, only for Youssuf Poulsen to equalize for RB Leipzig in the final minute (3–3, May 3, 2025). Arms crossed, biting his lip in rancour at the edge of the pitch, Kane must have had some very dark thoughts.

Despite his ten best-scorer titles—three of which have been in the Premier League and two in the Bundesliga—he remains incapable of winning a team trophy, despite ample opportunities: four defeats in four finals (two in the English Football League Cup, one in the 2019 Champions League with Tottenham, and one in the 2023 German Super Cup with Bayern) and two championship runner-up places (2017 Premier League and 2024 Bundesliga). The Three Lions captain hasn't had any greater success with the national side, losing two Euro finals: the first, at Wembley, against Italy (1–1, 2–3 on penalties) in 2021; the second, in Berlin, against Spain (1–2), in 2024.

The curse lifted on May 4, 2025, three months before he turned thirty-two, when Bayer Leverkusen was held to a draw by Freiburg SC (2–2). Lagging by eight points with just two days to go, the reigning champion couldn't catch Bayern. Kane therefore won his first title by proxy. Still, it was like a release. With classic British restraint, Kane posted a simple trophy emoji on X by way of celebration.

MUNICH (GERMANY), ALLIANZ ARENA
MAY 10, 2025
Harry Kane raises the solid silver Deutsche Meisterschale after Bayern Munich won the Bundesliga with a victory over Borussia Mönchengladbach (2–0).

2026
(home)

2026
(away)

2025
(home)

2025
(away)

2024
(home)

2022
(home)

2018
(home)

2015
(home)

2011
(home)

2001
(home)

1997
(home)

1995
(home)

1975
(away)

1974
(home)

1969
(home)

1967
(home)

1932
(home)

1902
(home)

"You'll never walk alone"

BEING PART OF THE RED ARMY, AS LIVERPOOL'S SUPPORTERS ARE KNOWN, IS A GUARANTEE OF NEVER HAVING TO WALK ALONE, AS EXPRESSED BY THE ANTHEM AND MOTTO OF THE MERSEYSIDE CLUB, FOUNDED IN 1892.

Players that pull on a Liverpool jersey are aware that they carry a heavy burden. They must honour the memory of the victims of the Heysel Stadium disaster, where 39 supporters died after fences and a retaining wall collapsed on May 29, 1985, and of the Hillsborough disaster, when 96 fans perished following a crush on standing terraces on April 15, 1989. Liverpool waited until 1896 to drop the blue and white sported by neighbours Everton and adopt a red jersey. The image of a liverbird, a mythical creature—half cormorant, half eagle—used to represent the city of Liverpool was added to the jersey in 1955, and then to the badge in 1987. The twin flames on either side symbolise the Hillsborough memorial outside Anfield. Since 1992, the club motto—"you'll never walk alone"—has appeared above the shield surrounding the liverbird.

13
GLOBAL HONOURS
6 UEFA Champions Leagues
3 UEFA Europa Leagues
4 UEFA Super Cups

54
NATIONAL HONOURS
20 English Leagues
8 FA Cups
10 English League Cups
16 Community Shields

2019
Champions League–winning jersey

Hot numbers

When Mohamed Salah signed with Liverpool FC on June 22, 2017, he didn't realise that this would provide a boon for the Royal Mail. You see, when the Egyptian player arrived at his new club, he insisted on retaining the number 11, with which he had launched his career over the two previous seasons at AS Roma. The problem was that Roberto Firmino had already been wearing this number for the past two years. Firmino's latest official jersey, bearing the famous 11, had already gone on sale to Liverpool fans in advance of the next season. Anxious to please a player they had just bought for $46.5 million on a five-year contract, the Reds asked Firmino to give up his lucky number. Firmino agreed, much to the joy of his new teammate. "I appreciate what Firmino did. I have to thank him very much. I like the number 11; it was my number in Rome and also the national team before," explained Salah.

But the club asked Firmino for another favour: to personally sign every shirt already sold with "Firmino 11" printed on it. Ever the gentleman, the Brazilian agreed. Although fans could not get their money back, they had until August 18, 2017 to send their shirts to Anfield "with a stamped self-addressed envelope big enough to contain [the] jersey. It will then be signed by Firmino and returned … ," announced the club.

In return, Firmino inherited the prestigious number 9, previously worn by legends of the Reds such as Ian Rush (1980–87, 1988–96) and Robbie Fowler (1995–2002, 2006–07). As for the Senegalese left-winger Sadio Mané, he swapped his 19 for the 10 in 2018—a number that does not hold the same legendary weight at Liverpool as it does at many other clubs. And it would be thanks to these three numbers (9, 10, and 11) that Liverpool won the sixth Champions League title in their rich history, against Tottenham, on June 1, 2019 (2–0).

LIVERPOOL (ENGLAND), ANFIELD
AUGUST 23, 2017
Mohamed Salah, scorer against Hoffenheim in the home leg of the Champions League (4–2; away: 2–1), is congratulated by Sadio Mané.

2026
(home)

2026
(away)

2025
(home)

2024
(away)

2021
(home)

2021
(away)

2017
(home)

2012
(third)

2005
(home)

2001
(away)

1996
(home)

1990
(home)

1981
(home)

1973
(home)

1963
(home)

1922
(away)

1896
(home)

1893
(home)

The Greek origins of Total Football

AJAX'S WHITE JERSEY WITH A BROAD RED STRIPE CONJURES UP MEMORIES—EVEN TODAY—OF SOME OF THE MOST ATTRACTIVE FOOTBALL EVER PLAYED.

Ajax's fabulous history began in 1893, when a group of friends established "Union," which would become FC Ajax one year later. But the club's official formation date is March 18, 1900, the day they joined the Amsterdam Football Association and established their home pitch in the east of the city, in the Jewish quarter. Since then, their more fanatical supporters call themselves the Joden ("Jews" in Dutch), although the club's roots can actually be traced back to Greek mythology rather than Judaism. A Trojan War hero, Ajax was known for his derring-do and bravery. His image has appeared on the club crest since September of 1928. So as to distinguish themselves from rivals PSV Eindhoven and Feyenoord, Ajax changed the colour of their jersey several times, having started out in black with a red sash around the waist. This was replaced by red and white stripes the day after their first league triumph in 1911. They subsequently opted for a white shirt with a wide, vertical red stripe in the middle of the jersey. It was this jersey that would later become the symbol of the "Total Football" approach preferred first by Rinus Michels and then Stefan Kovács.

11
GLOBAL HONOURS
4 UEFA Champions Leagues
1 UEFA Europa League
1 UEFA Cup Winners' Cup
3 UEFA Super Cups
2 Intercontinental Cups

65
NATIONAL HONOURS
36 Dutch Leagues
20 Dutch Cups
9 Dutch Super Cups

1992
Europa League–
winning jersey

Cruyff, from 9 to 14

One of the greatest players of all time, Johan Cruyff did not distinguish himself exclusively with his talent. He also stood out because of the number on the back of his jersey. Starting off with number 9, the "Prince of Amsterdam," his nickname in the city where his mother worked as a cleaner, became known from 1970 onwards for wearing 14, a number traditionally associated with the substitutes' bench. The reason for this unusual choice? While he was injured, his number 9 Netherlands shirt was passed on to Gerrie Mühren. Fully recovered and possibly a little angry at this turn of events, Cruyff did not ask to have the 9 returned to him, deciding to wear the 14 instead. But the tale did not end there. Famous for smoking cigarettes at halftime, he also distinguished himself from other players by slightly altering his kits. The Netherlands national side at the time wore Adidas shorts and an Adidas jersey with three black stripes down the sleeves. But not Cruyff. Having signed a separate sponsorship deal with Puma, the "Flying Dutchman" refused to wear a jersey manufactured by another brand, and played with just two stripes. This was not an issue during the 1978 World Cup as unfortunately Cruyff did not take part. Victim of a kidnap attempt at his Barcelona residence in 1977, he decided against accompanying his team-mates to Argentina, then run by a military dictatorship. The first player to win three European Footballer of the Year awards (1971, 1973 and 1974), Cruyff had nevertheless already earned his stripes in a remarkable career.

AMSTERDAM (NETHERLANDS), AMSTERDAM ARENA
NOVEMBER 7, 1978
Johan Cruyff wearing a special jersey during his farewell match with Ajax.

2026
(home)

2026
(away)

2024
(home)

2021
(home)

2021
(away)

2016
(home)

2016
(away)

2014
(home)

2011
(away)

2008
(home)

1995
(away)

1988
(home)

1983
(away)

1982
(home)

1980
(away)

1980
(home)

1958
(home)

1910
(home)

An Old Lady with an English dress sense

IT WAS THE RESULT OF A MISTAKE IN ENGLAND THAT LA VECCHIA SIGNORA GAVE UP HER PINK SHIRTS IN FAVOUR OF THE ICONIC STRIPES.

On November 1, 1897, thirteen young students met on a bench in Turin to establish a multi-sport club. Aged from 14 to 17, they called it "Sport Club Juventus" ("youth" in Latin). As football strips were not yet readily available, they started off playing in pink, with a tie (or bow tie) and black golf trousers. But as the shirts were of poor quality, they faded quickly. In 1903, they asked Nottingham Forest to deliver some of their red jerseys, but due to a mix-up, black and white striped Notts County FC tops were sent back to Italy instead, and Juventus have played in bianconeri colours ever since, considering them to be "aggressive and powerful." Juventus became powerful indeed on July 24, 1923, the day Edoardo Agnelli, son of Giovanni, founder of Fiat, purchased the club. Since then, the alliance between the Piedmont upper classes and the southern Italian workers in the Turin-based Fiat factories—who support the team—have enabled the club, renamed "Juventus Football Club" in 1945, to become La Fidanzata d'Italia ("The Girlfriend of Italy"). Yet Juventus' special relationship with England has not been forgotten. In 2011 to inaugurate their new stadium Juventus invited none other than Notts County FC, placed in the third tier of English football, for a friendly match to mark the occasion, an elegant gesture of gratitude for giving them their stripes.

JUVENTUS

10

GLOBAL HONOURS
2 UEFA Champions Leagues
3 UEFA Europa Leagues
1 UEFA Cup Winners' Cup
2 UEFA Super Cups
2 Intercontinental Cups

60

NATIONAL HONOURS
36 Italian Leagues
15 Italian Cups
9 Italian Super Cups

2015
Champions League–
runners-up jersey

Platini gave all he had

On May 17, 1987, after bidding farewell to 30,000 fans amassed in the dilapidated Stadio Comunale, Michel Platini headed off into the horizon following an exciting Juventus–Brescia clash (3–2), with good memories but without any of the jerseys he wore throughout his immense career. "I don't even have my last Juventus one," explains the former number 10, voted UEFA's President on January 26, 2007. "I really don't have any left at all, in fact. I've given them all away, to friends, to charitable organisations so that they can bring in some money, and to the many, many people who used to ask me when I was younger."

Platini did hold on to some objects, though. "In fact, I only held on to souvenirs that were round, like two of my three European Footballer of the Year [1983, 1984 and 1985] Ballon d'Or trophies. There's one at Mr Agnelli's house [Giovanni Agnelli, club president while Platini was at Juventus, who passed away on January 24, 2003]. The other two are at home; one's for my son, and the other's for my daughter. Mr Agnelli asked me one day: 'Is it really made out of gold?' I replied, 'Are you mad? I'd never have given it to you if it was! It's just a golden colour.' In return, he gave me a platinum one. The only thing that I kept that wasn't round is the Olympic torch from the Albertville winter games that I carried in 1992. I still have that in my possession."

Michel Platini wore the iconic jersey of Juventus FC from 1982 to 1987. His coach, Giovanni Trapattoni, said of the Frenchman: "He's a genius, a man born to play football."

2026
(home)

2026
(away)

2025
(home)

2024
(home)

2024
(away)

2023
(home)

2021
(home)

2020
(home)

2017
(home)

2010
(away)

2006
(home)

2006
(away)

1995
(away)

1991
(home)

1987
(away)

1983
(away)

1932
(home)

1897
(home)

International outlook

FOUNDED BY DISSENTING VOICES FROM AC MILAN WHO DISAGREED WITH THE CLUB'S REFUSAL TO FIELD FOREIGNERS, INTERNAZIONALE SUFFERED BETWEEN THE WARS UNDER ITALY'S FASCIST REGIME.

Established on March 9, 1908 at the Orologio restaurant by former members of AC Milan, Internazionale got its name from the desire of its founders to allow foreign players to join the newly formed team. Milan's refusal to let the 44 Italian and Swiss dissidents play was the principal reason behind their decision to leave the club in order to start up their own. Inter Milan lost their original colours of black and blue in 1928, when the fascist regime, which had prohibited towns from having more than one club, forced them to merge with US Milanese to create an entity known as Ambrosiana, after St Ambrose, the patron saint of Milan. After a 17-year period during which they wore a white jersey with a red cross (the city emblem) they reverted to their original name and colours in 1945. The white shirt would get one more airing, however, as it was used during the 2007–2008 season to celebrate Internazionale's centenary. In 1967, they added a star above the club badge, honouring their ten Italian League titles. Then a second one, after obtaining his twentieth title, in 2024. In May 2011, the iconic jersey became the first football shirt to go into space, when astronaut Paolo Nespoli took it with him on a mission. From international to interplanetary . . .

9
GLOBAL HONOURS
3 UEFA Champions Leagues
3 UEFA Europa Leagues
3 Intercontinental Cups

37
NATIONAL HONOURS
20 Italian Leagues
9 Italian Cups
8 Italian Super Cups

2010
Champions League–,
Italian Cup–, and
Italian League–
winning jersey

Unlucky yellow

Not being the "home" team, Inter Milan were unable to wear their traditional blue and black strip for the Champions League final at Munich's Allianz Arena on May 31, 2025. The reason was the predominantly blue shirt worn by Paris Saint-Germain. The Nerazzurri should have worn their white away strip for this first ever Inter–PSG match, but they made the surprising choice to wear their third kit: yellow with black detailing, inspired by Milanese architecture and design.

Yellow is not simply eye-catching, it is associated with nobility, wealth, and even spiritual elevation in certain civilizations. It exudes light and warmth, as well as symbolizing personal power, logic, and humour. It is the colour of movement and energy. But Inter didn't wear yellow for its symbolism. They wore it for superstitious reasons. The only Champions League match they had lost that season (out of sixteen played) was while wearing white (0–1 to Bayer Leverkusen on December 19, 2024). They had, however, won both of the matches they played in yellow (1–0 against Sparta Prague and 2–0 against Feyenoord Rotterdam) plus five victories out of seven matches in Serie A. What they had forgotten was that yellow is also the colour of misfortune. Bullfighters never wear it. Becoming the first Champions League finalist to wear their third kit was not a successful move. Inter suffered the heaviest defeat (0–5) in 70 Champions League finals, making this the fourth successive defeat of an Italian team in a Champions League final since Inter beat Bayern Munich 2–0 in 2010 wearing . . . nerazzurro.

MUNICH (GERMANY), ALLIANZ ARENA
MAY 31, 2025
Inter Milan captain Lautaro Martinez leaves the pitch with his head bowed after losing the Champions League final to Paris Saint-Germain (0–5).

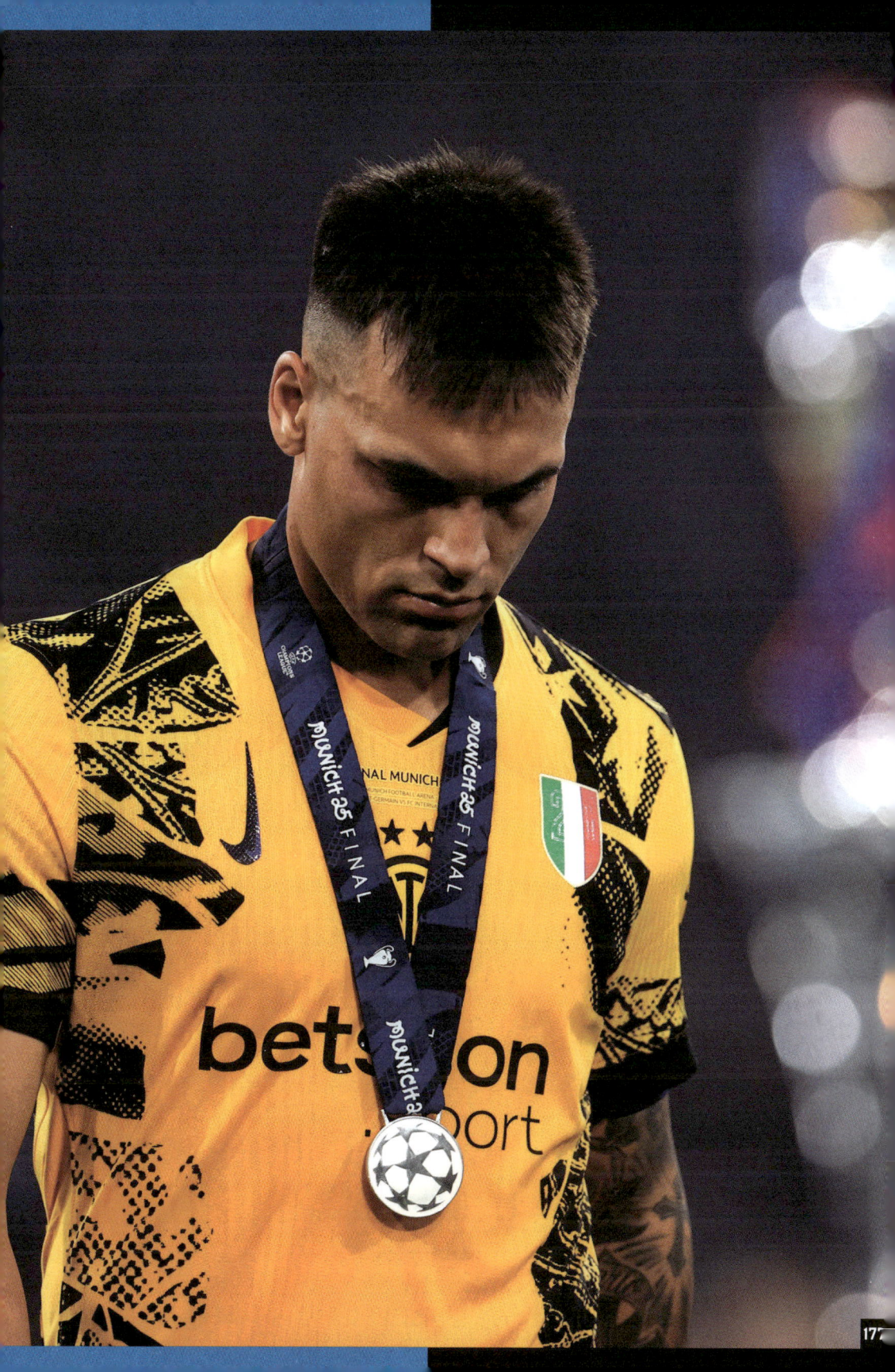

2026
(home)

2026
(away)

2025
(home)

2024
(home)

2024
(away)

2021
(home)

2021
(away)

2020
(home)

2017
(home)

1998
(third)

1996
(away)

1989
(home)

1981
(home)

1971
(home)

1965
(away)

1964
(away)

1929
(home)

1910
(home)

The Red Devils, still in Heaven

ALTHOUGH THEIR GAME HAS BEEN SOMEWHAT IN DECLINE SINCE THEIR EMBLEMATIC MANAGER, SIR ALEX FERGUSON, MANCHESTER UNITED CONTINUE TO BE A FLOURISHING CONCERN.

Newton Heath LYR FC, which was founded in 1878 by the employees of a regional railroad company, changed its green-and-gold colours to a red shirt and white shorts in 1902 when it became Manchester United FC. Having learned that the neighbouring rugby league club, Salford, had been nicknamed the Red Devils during a tour to France in the 1930s, Manchester United's manager, Sir Matt Busby, decided to bestow this intimidating moniker on his Busby Babes.

Since the early 1970s, a red devil armed with a trident has been the centre of the coat of arms of a club that seems to have fallen back into line, after taking thirteen of the twenty Premier League titles and two of the three UEFA Champions League titles it won between 1993 and 2013. The club has been controlled by an American family, the Glazers, since May 12, 2005, but despite a record turnover ($880M), Manchester United ended the 2023–2024 season with heavy financial losses ($150M) for the fifth year running. And they came up short on the pitch, too, losing the Europa League 1–0 to Tottenham on May 21, 2025.

8
GLOBAL HONOURS
3 UEFA Champions Leagues
1 UEFA Cup Winners' Cup
1 UEFA Super Cup
1 Intercontinental Cup
2 FIFA Club World Cup

60
NATIONAL HONOURS
20 English Leagues
13 FA Cups
6 English League Cups
21 Community Shields

FINAL MOSCOW 2008
21st MAY-LUZHNIKI STADIUM

AIG

2008
Champions League–
winning jersey

MARADONA GOOD
PELĒ BETTER
GEORGE BEST

Beckham cannot kick with his left foot, can't head the ball, can't tackle and he doesn't score enough goals. Otherwise he's all right.

If I had been born ugly, you would have never heard of Pelé

In 1969, I gave up women and alcohol. It was the worst 20 minutes of my life.

" I SPENT A LOT OF MONEY ON BOOZE, BIRDS, AND FAST CARS. THE REST I JUST SQUANDERED. "

The legend of number 7

It all started in 1961, when Manchester United scout Bob Bishop unearthed a talented 15-year-old by the name of George Best. It took just one training session for the club to sign him. Seven years and six trophies later, Best was named European Footballer of the Year for 1968, and the legend of number 7 was born. The phenomenon went far beyond the scope of football. Capable of absolutely anything on, as well as off, the pitch, the gifted winger was the first true rock star footballer of his era. Ousted by United in 1974, he lapsed into alcoholism, suffered financial ruin and died on November 25, 2005 at the age of 59. A one-time idol of Maradona, Best was given a grand, near-state funeral in Belfast. Bryan Robson then wore the 7 jersey from 1981–1994, before Eric Cantona, the enfant terrible exiled from France, revived the legend. Following the sudden retirement of the "King," who was voted best United player of all time by the fans, David Beckham inherited the number. Beckham would in turn hand it down to Cristiano Ronaldo in 2003. When the Portuguese striker joined Real Madrid in 2009, Michael Owen, the 2001 European Footballer of the Year, donned the jersey, but enjoyed less success. Just like the Argentinian Angel Di Maria, the Dutchman Memphis Depay, the Chilean Alexis Sanchez and the Uruguayan Edinson Cavani. The refusal of Japanese international Shinji Kagawa to wear it last year led to Ecuadorian winger Antonio Valencia taking up the mantle. Manchester United fans, however, would love to see a new George Best restore the brilliance of the legendary number 7.

Eric Cantona, affectionately known by Manchester United fans as "King Eric."

2026
(home)

2025
(third)

2024
(home)

2024
(away)

2017
(home)

2017
(away)

2013
(home)

2013
(third)

2010
(home)

1999
(home)

1998
(home)

1996
(away)

1994
(home)

1980
(away)

1980
(home)

1968
(third)

1909
(home)

1903
(home)

How the Pensioners became champions

LONG VIEWED AS ALSO-RANS IN THE ENGLISH GAME, CHELSEA HAVE BECOME ONE OF THE MOST POWERFUL CLUBS IN THE WORLD.

When property developers renovated Stamford Bridge in 1904, they had planned for every eventuality, except local team Fulham's refusal to play there. Forced to conjure up a resident club, they bestowed the name of the adjacent borough on it, and so Chelsea FC was born on March 10, 1905. Bluish-green jerseys, taken from the colours of the stable belonging to then chairman the Earl of Cadogan, were chosen. The colours became royal blue in 1912. The club emblem, meanwhile, was modified no fewer than seven times. Originally, a Chelsea Pensioner (the term for former members of the British army housed in a nearby nursing home, the Royal Hospital Chelsea) was depicted on the crest. But the image was removed in 1952, when the "Pensioners" became known as the "Blues." A year later, drawing inspiration from the coat of arms of the Metropolitan Borough of Chelsea, Cadogan's own coat of arms, and that of the former Lords of the Manor of Chelsea, a backwards-facing blue lion holding a staff was added to the jersey. A more realistic lion was used between 1986 and 2005, the club's centenary year. Following the takeover by Russian billionaire Roman Abramovich on July 2, 2003, the crest reverted to the traditional lion, a symbol of the past and of a rosy-looking future.

10
GLOBAL HONOURS
2 UEFA Champions League
2 UEFA Europa League
2 UEFA Cup Winners' Cups
2 UEFA Super Cup
1 UEFA Conference League
1 FIFA Club World Cup

23
NATIONAL HONOURS
6 English Leagues
8 FA Cups
5 League Cups
4 Community Shields

adidas

CHELSEA
FOOTBALL CLUB

FINAL MUNICH 2012
19ᵗʰ MAY FUSSBALL ARENA MÜNCHEN
FC BAYERN MÜNCHEN vs CHELSEA FC

SAMSUNG

2012
Champions League–
winning jersey

Drogba, a fan of the Blues

A massive portrait of Didier Drogba looks down on the Shed End, the historic wall that supports the south side of Stamford Bridge. It shows him kissing the Chelsea badge on the Allianz Arena pitch, the stage for the Blues' greatest achievement: their capture of the Champions League. It was Drogba who almost single-handedly delivered the mythical trophy to the Chelsea fans on May 19, 2012, equalising with a header in the 88th minute, then putting away his team's last penalty kick in the ensuing shootout against Bayern Munich (1–1, 4–3 on penalties). The image guarantees the Ivorian's eternal presence in the hearts of the London club's supporters. On November 2, 2012, they even voted him the greatest Chelsea player of all time, ahead of living legends such as Frank Lampard, Gianfranco Zola and John Terry. And yet the relationship between Drogba and Chelsea's fan-base got off to a rocky start in 2004, as the latter held the former's initial reluctance about joining the club against him for a long period. This would explain why his number 15 jersey, and then his 11 (picked up by Brazilian midfielder Oscar in 2012), sold in fewer numbers than those of Lampard or Terry, despite the African striker's habit of buying hundreds of them at the club shop to send back to Abidjan. He was not a collector, though. "I've only got three jerseys framed at home: Zidane's, Ronaldo's and Ronaldinho's," he once said. Drogba would have very much liked to add Messi's to his wall before leaving European football, but after having promised him his shirt before the semifinal of the 2012 Champions League, (2–2, April 24. First leg: 1–0), the Argentinian made a sharp exit as soon as the final whistle sounded. Drogba was likely consoled by the fact that T-shirts featuring his own image still sell like hotcakes in Chelsea's shop. He no longer needs to buy them up himself. With their victory against Real Betis in the Conference League final (4-1) on May 28, 2025, Chelsea became the first team to win all four European Cups.

MUNICH (GERMANY), ALLIANZ ARENA
MAY 19, 2012
Scorer of Chelsea's equaliser and their last penalty kick in the shootout of the final against Bayern, Ivorian striker Didier Drogba clutches the London club's first Champions League trophy.

2026
(home)

2026
(away)

2025
(home)

2022
(away)

2022
(home)

2021
(third)

2019
(home)

2013
(away)

2012
(home)

2004
(home)

2004
(away)

1998
(home)

1991
(home)

1991
(away)

1985
(home)

1976
(away)

1955
(home)

1905
(home)

The Santos spotlight

FROM PELÉ TO NEYMAR, SANTOS HAS PROVIDED A PLATFORM FOR A HOST OF ICONIC PERFORMERS THROUGH THE YEARS. THIS REPUTATION EARNED THE CLUB A FIFTH-PLACED RANKING IN THE FIFA CLUB OF THE CENTURY VOTING IN DECEMBER 2000.

When three men met above a bakery on April 14, 1912 with the intention of forming another football club in São Paulo state, they had no way of knowing they were making history. Santos Futebol Clube, created on that fateful day, would go on to produce and nurture such magicians of the beautiful game as Pelé, Robinho, and Neymar.

One of the founders' first tasks was to select a colour for their new club's jersey. His first choice was a shirt with white, blue and gold stripes. But as it proved too complicated to make at the time, Santos opted from March 31, 1913 for black and white stripes, like the ones used at Juventus. Over time, though, they settled on an all-white strip. A third, turquoise jersey was also worn in 2012 to mark the club's centenary. The town of Santos is located near the city of São Paulo, Brazil's economic heart, and boasts the country's largest seaport. For this reason, the club's founders decided to adopt a sea creature, a whale, as its mascot. Although it does not appear on the club crest, Pelé's former employers have long been nicknamed the Peixe ("Fish").

7
GLOBAL HONOURS
3 Copas Libertadores
1 Copa CONMEBOL
1 Recopa Sudamericana
2 Intercontinental Cups

36
NATIONAL HONOURS
8 Brazilian Leagues
22 Campeonatos Paulista
1 Brazilian Cup
5 Torneios Rio – São Paulo

2011
Copa Libertadores–
winning jersey

Neymar, in Pelé's shoes

This time, the return of the Prince took place with the number of the King. Previously, Neymar had never played for Santos with Pelé's number 10. When he started out in seniors (2009–2013) at the club that trained him, Neymar was happy to make do with number 11, helping Santos FC to win its last big victories: Copa do Brasil in 2010, Copa Libertadores in 2011, and the South American Cup Winners Cup in 2012. Neymar had let his compatriots Ganso and Renato Abreu wear the legendary 10. Likewise at FC Barcelona (2013–2017), where it belonged to Lionel Messi. But he has always worn number 10 for the Seleçao, since his first cap in 2012.

Santos announced the news in a video published on social media on January 31, 2025 (day of the official announcement of the Prince's return): the number 10 would be attributed to Neymar. Over a montage of images retracing his career with Santos, Neymar talked about the iconic number 10 made famous by "O Rei" sixty years earlier: "King Pelé, your will is my command. The throne and the crown will always be yours, because you are eternal. But the number 10 . . . It will be an honour to wear the Sacred Shirt that represents so much for Santos and for the world. I promise to do all I can to continue to honour your legend, King." From the start of the 2024–2025 season, the number 10 was worn by Tomas Rincon, João Schmidt, and Guilherme, who celebrated his goal, not long before the return of the prodigal son, by imitating Neymar's dance.

**BRAGANZA (BRAZIL),
ESTÁDIO CÍCERO DE SOUZA MARQUES**
MAY 29, 2025
Neymar during a friendly match against the German club RB Leipzig (1–3).

2025
(home)

2025
(away)

2024
(third)

2022
(home)

2022
(away)

2021
(home)

2020
(third)

2018
(home)

2013
(home)

2012
(away)

2009
(home)

2009
(third)

1995
(home)

1992
(away)

1990
(home)

1975
(away)

1963
(home)

1912
(home)

The Dragon, a living myth

PORTUGAL'S BIGGEST CLUB USES THE LEGENDARY DRAGON, WHICH GIVES ITS NAME TO THEIR STADIUM, TO STRIKE FEAR IN THE HEARTS OF OPPONENTS.

Founded on September 28, 1893, Futebol Clube do Porto rose to true prominence in 1904 to become Portugal's most successful club. The blue and white colours stem from the desire of those in charge in the early days to bestow their multi-sport club with a strong national identity. To achieve that, they borrowed the colours from the Portuguese royal flag. Originally, the crest was comprised of a blue ball bearing the initials of the name of the club (FCP), to which the coat of arms of the city of Porto was added in 1922 to symbolise the strong bond between club and city. Above sits a dragon on the city walls, defending it from potential invaders. The dragon mythology relays the idea that the inhabitants of Porto never give up and remain motivated by a spirit of conquest. This symbolism is so far-reaching that when the club's new stadium opened on November 16, 2003, it was christened "Estádio do Dragão" (Dragon Stadium). "A Chama do Dragão" (the flame of the dragon) has ever since enabled FC Porto to shine brightly in the domestic league as well as in Europe.

7
GLOBAL HONOURS
2 UEFA Champions Leagues
2 UEFA Europa Leagues
1 UEFA Super Cup
2 Intercontinental Cups

75
NATIONAL HONOURS
30 Portuguese Leagues
20 Portuguese Cups
24 Portuguese Super Cups
1 Portuguese League Cup

2004
Champions League–
winning jersey

Rabah Madjer, eight's the one

Rabah Madjer was still an unknown in Portugal when he arrived at FC Porto in 1985. Having come via Racing Paris and FC Tours, the Portuguese called him "The Frenchman," even though he was born in Algiers. The club gave him the number 8, that of a box-to-box midfielder, which was odd for such a creative player, forged in the image of his idol, Johan Cruyff. It didn't bother him, though. Indeed, despite always wearing the number 11 for Algeria, he would keep the number 8 throughout the rest of his club career. He would even retain it when on loan to Valencia, after having written the number large in the history of the Dragons. Madjer took FC Porto to the top of Europe, on that magical evening of May 27, 1987, in Vienna. Lagging 1–0 to the Bayern Munich of Lothar Matthäus and Andreas Brehme, he equalised in the 78th minute with a genius backheel off a Juary pass. His instinctive kick from his right foot, with his back to the goal, dramatically changed the outcome of this European Cup final and the destiny of his club. Two minutes later, it was him who made a decisive pass to Juary, and with it, FC Porto's first European title (2–1). Madjer's name would be forever linked with that backheel kick, in the same manner that the Czechoslovak Antonín Panenka would lend his name to the penalty flick he pulled off against the German goalkeeper Sepp Maier in the penalty shootout that decided the Euro 1976 final in Czechoslovakia's favour (2–2, 5–3 on penalties). In 1987, still bearing the number 8 on his back, the Algerian was a scorer and decisive passer in the Intercontinental Cup against Peñarol (2–1, on December 13, 1987), earning him the African Ballon d'Or.

VIENNA (AUSTRIA), ERNST-HAPPEL STADION
MAY 27, 1987
Rabah Madjer lifts and kisses the Champions League trophy after scoring a goal and making a decisive pass against Bayern Munich (2–1).

2026

(home)

2026

(away)

2025

(home)

2025

(away)

2024

(home)

2024

(away)

2021

(home)

2020

(away)

2018

(home)

2013
(home)

2012
(away)

2009
(home)

2004
(away)

2002
(home)

2001
(away)

1988
(home)

1980
(home)

1907
(home)

The crazy gang

CLUB OF THE STARS (GARRINCHA, RIVELINO, SÓCRATES, AND RONALDO, AMONG OTHERS), CORINTHIANS OCCUPIES A SPECIAL PLACE IN THE HEART AND HISTORY OF THE BRAZILIAN PEOPLE.

When immigrant workers from southern Europe established the club on September 1, 1910, they decided to name it after the touring team from London that had just won six matches on Brazilian soil. And so Sport Club Corinthians Paulista came into being. The largest multi-sport club in São Paulo, it is also one of the most popular. Corinthians claim to have 35 million fans, including former President of Brazil Lula (2003–2011) and Formula 1 drivers Rubens Barrichello and Ayrton Senna (who died in 1994). Their mission statement promises that they will be the team "of the people, by the people and for the people." Although their supporters are nicknamed "O bando de Loucos" ("the crazy gang"), their first administrators were rather conservative, choosing a cream-coloured jersey, which would eventually become white over time. It was not until 1954 that the black shirt with thin white stripes made an appearance. As for the crest, although it dates from 1913, it has been touched up since. The current emblem stretches back to 1940, when an anchor and two oars were added to reflect the club's success in nautical sports.

4

GLOBAL HONOURS
1 Copa Libertadores
2 FIFA Club World Cups
1 Recopa Sudamericana

47

NATIONAL HONOURS
7 Brazilian Leagues
31 Campeonatos Paulista
3 Brazilian Cups
1 Brazilian Super Cup
5 Torneios Rio – São Paulo

2012
Copa Libertadores–
winning jersey

A very democratic jersey

Putting on a Corinthians jersey at the start of the 1980s was not a trivial matter. It was a political choice. That was the intent of Brazil captain Sócrates, one of the founders of the Corinthians Democracy initiative in November 1981. This ideological movement was launched to challenge the military dictatorship and to offer the players the opportunity to run the club collectively. Gate receipts and TV rights were distributed between all the club's employees and between the players, under the guise of win bonuses. In return, they made the decisions about player recruitment and new coaches, which occurred when Zé Maria, former Corinthians defender and 1970 World Cup winner, was offered the manager's post. They also walked onto the pitch before the final of the 1983 São Paulo State Championship to unfurl a banner which read: "Win or lose, but always within a democracy." This self-management, married to an entertaining brand of football, helped the club enjoy great success both on and off the pitch. "We were fighting for freedom, for a change in our country," explained Sócrates, who sadly passed away on December 4, 2011 at the age of 57. A qualified doctor of medicine with a strong political conscience, and the elder brother of Raï, also a one-time Seleçao skipper, Sócrates would often appear on the pitch with the inscription "Democracia Corinthiana" on his jersey, or with messages on his back encouraging people to vote in elections. This mini-republic came to a natural end with the emergence of democracy in Brazil in 1985.

Sócrates celebrates a goal during the Clássico Majestoso between Corinthians and São Paulo in 1982 (right). Much more than a gifted footballer, the "Doctor" was also a man of unshakable political convictions often displayed on his shirt (below).

2024
(home)

2024
(away)

2019
(home)

2016
(home)

2013
(home)

2012
(home)

2010
(home)

1998
(home)

1994
(home)

1974
(home)

1970
(home)

1962
(home)

1958
(home)

1958
(away)

1950
(home)

1949
(home)

1930
(home)

1917-1919
(home)

Starry mattress makers

MADRID'S SECOND CLUB TOOK THE COLOURS USED IN MATTRESS MAKING, AS WELL AS THE CITY'S SYMBOLS (NOTABLY THE CONSTELLATION URSA MAJOR), TO FORGE ITS IDENTITY.

The club was founded on April 26, 1903, by three Basque students living in Madrid, in homage to the Athletic Bilbao from their childhoods. The original uniform was borrowed from the same blue-and-white stripes of Blackburn Rovers FC's jersey, but on a trip to England in 1911, one of the members of the board was unable to find any spare Rovers kit and brought back some Southampton shirts instead. Luckily, red-and-white striped material was already commonly used in Spanish mattresses (colchónes)—and had the added bonus of costing less to produce—hence the club's nicknames of Los Colchoneros (the Mattress Makers) and Los Rojiblancos (the Red and White). Missing from the team's original coat of arms were the bear and the strawberry tree—symbols of Madrid—which were added in 1917. Similarly, the seven white stars evoked both the constellation Ursa Major and the flag of the autonomous community of Madrid. Despite this strong local identity, Atlético remained in the shadow of Real Madrid for a long time until the return of its Argentinian former midfielder Diego Simeone in 2011 as its manager. The club is also known as Los Indios (the Indians), a moniker that may derive from the traditionally strong South American contingent among Atlético's mainly working-class fans, or else the fact that in colonial times, the Indians were the enemies of Los Blancos (the Whites)—nickname of Atlético's rivals, Real Madrid FC.

8
GLOBAL HONOURS
1 UEFA Cup Winners' Cup
3 UEFA Europa Leagues
3 UEFA Super Cups
1 FIFA Club World Cup

23
NATIONAL HONOURS
11 Spanish Leagues
10 Spanish Cups
2 Spanish Super Cups

2014
Spanish League–
winning jersey, and
Champions League–
runners-up jersey

Griezmann, for the love of Beckham

An apostle of the beautiful game, Antoine Griezmann only acknowledges one god in football—David Beckham—to such an extent that he often changes his hairstyle to mimic his childhood hero. He also copies his English idol by insisting on long-sleeved shirts, whatever the weather, and on wearing the number 7 whenever he can, including for the French team.

There have been two instances in his glorious career when he has had to let his favourite number go. The first was when he arrived at FC Barcelona in 2019 and had to make do with adding a 1 in front of the 7, before getting it back for the following two seasons. The second was when he returned to Atlético de Madrid in 2021—when number 7 was worn by the Portuguese player Joao Felix. So "Grizou" picked number 8, for two reasons. Firstly, it was the number worn by LA Lakers star Kobe Bryant (of whom he was a huge fan) during the first three of his five NBA titles (1996–2006). Secondly, April 8 was the day his wife Erika Choperena gave birth to their three children—daughter Mia (2016), son Amaro (2019), and little Alba (2021)—not to mention that the sculptor Stéphane Barret, who made the wax statue of Grizou for the Musée Grévin in Paris, was also born on April 8. "It wasn't intentional, or done on purpose, it just happened, but it's also a day enshrined forever in our family, particularly between brothers and sisters," Griezmann says with a smile. "I have no magic spell to explain such a thing except to say that when you're on vacation, nice and relaxed, with no pressure, no match or training session, things happen naturally." And it was just as naturally that he took back number 7 from Joao Felix when the latter left for Chelsea in 2023.

MADRID (SPAIN), RIYADH AIR METROPOLITANO
OCTOBER 20, 2024, 81ST MINUTE
Antoine Griezmann raises a triumphant fist after scoring to take Atlético de Madrid ahead of Leganés (3–1).

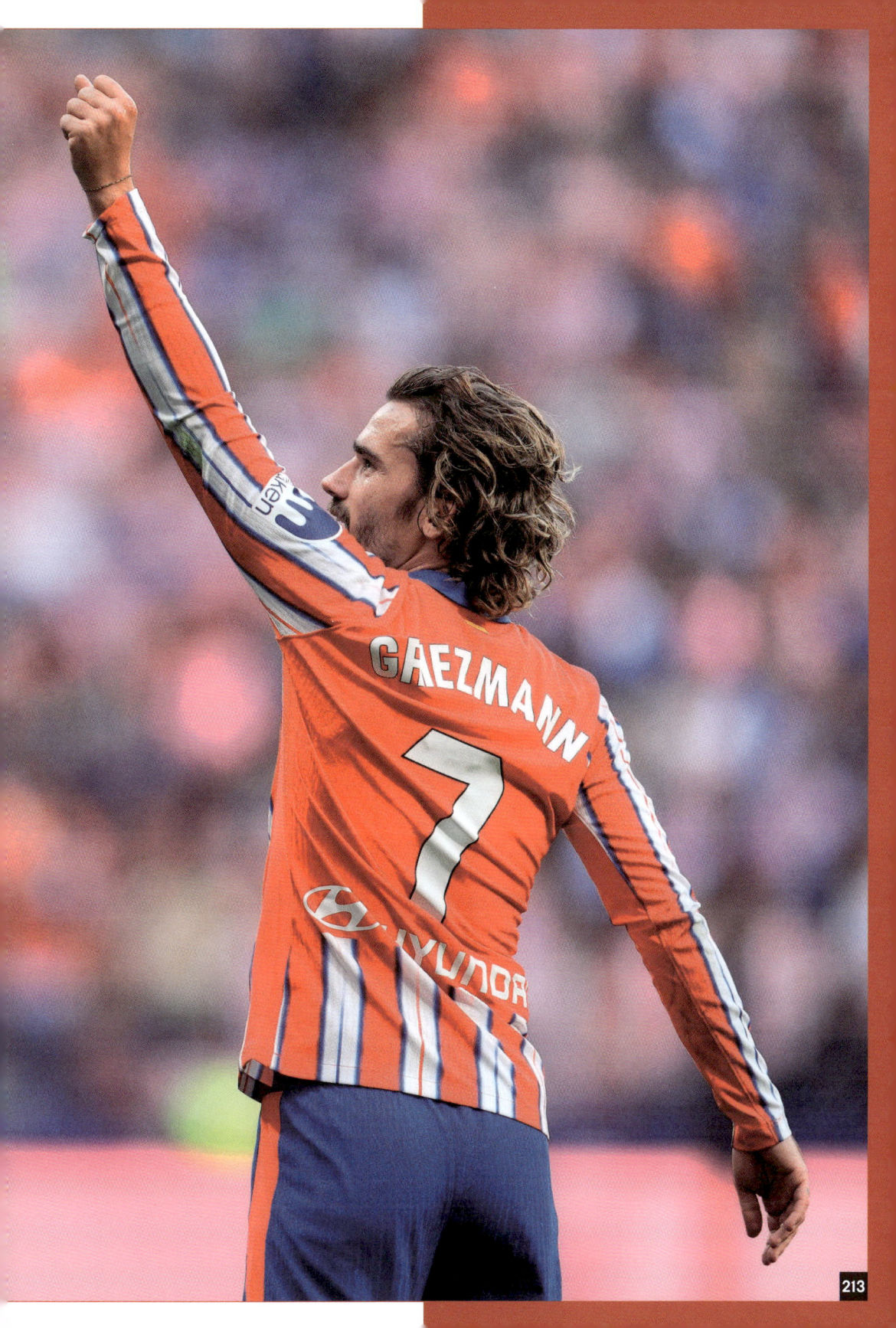

2026
(home)

2026
(away)

2025
(home)

2024
(home)

2024
(away)

2023
(home)

2022
(home)

2020
(home)

2019
(away)

2016
(home)

2015
(away)

2007
(home)

2006
(away)

1999
(away)

1984
(home)

1951
(away)

1949
(home)

1904
(home)

The 200,000 member club

FLOATED ON THE STOCK EXCHANGE SINCE MAY 22, 2007 (15 MILLION SHARES), BENFICA, ONE OF LISBON'S TWO GIANT CLUBS ALONGSIDE SPORTING, BOAST A LEVEL OF POPULAR SUPPORT IN PORTUGAL THAT ONLY PORTO COME CLOSE TO.

On February 28, 1904, 24 students formed a multi-sport club at the Franco pharmacy on the Rua de Belém, in the south-west of Lisbon. Naming it "Benfica," after one of the city's civil parishes, they decided the team would wear red and white. Their motto—"E Pluribus Unum" ("Out of many, one")—was inscribed on the crest, which took the shape of a bicycle wheel (cycling being another sport practised at the Benfica club) surrounding a red and white shield. The same motto also happens to appear on the Great Seal of the United States. Over a century later, on September 29, 2009, Benfica registered its 200,000th sócio (paying member) across the world. In the meantime, after having abandoned their policy of only signing Portuguese players in the 1970s, they placed three stars above the club crest, representing the 30th Portuguese League title, attained in 1994. They won their first championship back in 1936, and now have about seventy trophies in their display cabinet.

2
GLOBAL HONOURS
2 UEFA Champions Leagues

84
NATIONAL HONOURS
38 Portuguese Leagues
26 Portuguese Cups
8 Portuguese League Cups
9 Portuguese Super Cups
3 Campeonato de Portugal

2010
Portuguese League–
winning jersey

Where eagles dare

The animal world has often inspired club founders pondering over potential crests. A basic method of communication, the chosen beast—often ravenous, carnivorous or wild—is meant to embody the values of a club. Benfica settled on an Iberian Eagle, which symbolises authority, independence and nobility. An eagle named Vitoria ("Victory") is actually released over the Estádio da Luz prior to each home fixture, and is depicted with its wings wide open on the club crest. Benfica are not alone in using an eagle in this way. Italian outfit Lazio do the same before their matches at Rome's Stadio Olimpico, while Palermo's badge displays the white and gold eagle from the town's coat of arms. In Greece, the bird finds itself in great demand. Emblem of the Ecumenical Patriarchate of Constantinople, it figures on the crests of AEK Athens, PAOK Salonika and Doxa Drama. In Turkey, Besiktas eagle is black, like the black on the club's jersey. The same goes for Nice in France, for Pirin Blagoevgrad in Bulgaria and for Spartak Nalchik in Russia, but not for their compatriots of Sibir Novosibirsk, who prefer a blue eagle, as do Crystal Palace (England). Eintracht Frankfurt's eagle is red, while in the Ivory Coast (Africa Sports National), Hungary (Ferencváros) and Morocco (Raja Casablanca), the bird is green. Mexican heavyweights Club América boast a golden eagle, and Manchester City's has its tongue sticking out. National teams are also not averse to using the large bird of prey as a symbol. Mali ("The Eagles") and Tunisia ("The Eagles of Carthage") are just two examples. What all of these jerseys have in common is that their fans are unsympathetic to any attempts to remove the powerful image. When Poland's kit manufacturer replaced their eagle with a less visible variant of the national emblem, fan protests forced them to put it back in its rightful place ahead of Euro 2012, the competition that Poland co-hosted with Ukraine.

"Águia Vitória," the eagle that soars above the stands prior to each match held at the Estádio da Luz, has appeared on the Benfica crest for over a hundred years.

2026
(home)

2026
(away)

2024
(home)

2024
(away)

2023
(home)

2023
(away)

2021
(home)

2021
(away)

2021
(third)

2015
(home)

2012
(away)

2007
(home)

2005
(home)

1999
(away)

1973
(home)

1961
(away)

1935
(home)

1904
(home)

A citizen's club

FOUNDED BY A VICAR'S WIFE WITH SOCIAL AIMS, MANCHESTER'S SECOND CLUB CONSIDERS ITSELF TO BE THE CLUB OF THE CITY'S INHABITANTS, HENCE ITS NICKNAME: THE CITIZENS.

Anna Connell, the wife of the vicar of St Mark's parish, was concerned at seeing the youth of West Gorton spending their money in the pubs. So, in 1880, she decided to encourage them to play sports by starting a cricket club, followed by a football club. The players of St Mark's FC initially wore black shirts stamped with Maltese crosses, white shorts, and black-and-white–striped socks. The colour blue first appeared in 1887, when the kit was a white shirt with dark blue stripes (later changed to light blue). The club was first called St Mark's Gorton, and underwent two name changes before going bankrupt and definitively taking the name Manchester City FC on April 16, 1894. The strip changed again to a sky-blue shirt—known as Cambridge blue—with white shorts and dark blue socks. The seventh, and most recent, club badge (introduced in 2016) still features the city's coat of arms, but the golden eagle, a key element of the 1997 badge, was replaced by a ship symbolising the Manchester Ship Canal. The baby blue of the water the ship sails on is crossed by three light blue diagonals that represent Manchester's three rivers, emblazoned with a Lancashire rose.

4
GLOBAL HONOURS
1 UEFA Champions League
1 UEFA Super Cup
1 FIFA Club World Cup
1 UEFA Cup Winners' Cup

32
NATIONAL HONOURS
10 English Leagues
7 FA Cups
8 League Cups
7 Community Shields

2023
Champions League–
winning jersey

Haaland, 9 is the magic number

An exceptional scorer, Erling Haaland knows how to count. And not just the impressive number of his goals. He has also used numbers to build a career worthy of his talent. The date of his transfer to Manchester City—June 13, 2022—matches the day his father, Alf-Inge Häland, signed with the Citizens: June 13, 2000. After replacing the Norwegian "ä" with "aa" to make it easier for the foreign media to write his name, Haaland also realised that to make it as a football star, he needed to play with the number 9. Seeing him with his father's 15—a number not in use when he arrived at Man City—would have carried too much symbolism. So Haaland junior did all he could to get the number 9. After starting with number 19 at Bryne FK, he had to make do with number 30 at other clubs, except at Borussia Dortmund, where he obtained number 17 in December 2019 in homage to Pierre-Emerick Aubameyang, BVB's top foreign scorer. From then on he took number 9, including for the national team, starting from March 25, 2022 when, against Slovakia (2–0), the Norwegian Football Federation (NFF) asked Alexander Sørloth to add a 1 before his 9 so that Haaland could take number 9, having been obliged to play with 23 on his back. Ståle Solbakken, their coach, was clear about the reason: "He really wants it and there's a major commercial aspect. Erling is already a big brand and he will remain so for many years. Him and the NFF can take advantage of it." It also seemed unthinkable that he wouldn't wear the 9 at City, even though Gabriel Jesus had it. Three days after the Norwegian's arrival, the Brazilian left for Arsenal.

MANCHESTER (ENGLAND), ETIHAD STADIUM
OCTOBER 2, 2022
Erling Haaland has flown through the Premier League since arriving at the Citizens in 2022.

2026
(home)

2025
(away)

2025
(home)

2025
(third)

2024
(home)

2023
(away)

2021
(home)

2021
(away)

2016
(third)

2016
(away)

2013
(home)

2012
(away)

2012
(home)

2011
(third)

1980
(home)

1956
(away)

1937
(home)

1884
(home)

Proud as a rooster

FOUNDED IN 1882, TOTTENHAM DRAWS ON THE NOBILITY AND BRAVERY (AND SPURS) OF THE ROOSTER, WHICH HAS, SINCE 1921, ADORNED ITS CREST.

When the students of All Hallows Church, North London, decided to found a football club in 1882, they realized that a descendant of Henry Percy (a noble-man who had led the rebellion against King Henry IV of England in 1403) lived in the area. Henry Percy was dubbed Harry Hotspur, owing to his impulsive character, his speed when advancing, and his readiness to attack. He plays a major role in William Shakespeare's play *Henry IV*. In homage, the students named themselves the Spurs and called their club Hotspur FC. In 1884, it became Tottenham Hotspur Football Club (taking the name of its multiethnic neighborhood), to differentiate itself from another team, which was named London Hotspur.

In 1909, William James Scott, a former player, decided to erect a huge statue of a rooster, with spurs on its ankles, standing atop a ball above the West Stand at White Hart Lane Stadium. This became the club's emblem in 1921, and the rooster now proudly overlooks the Tottenham Hotspur Stadium, which was opened on April 3, 2019. The logo also appears on the club strip—which became white in 1899 in homage to Preston North End FC, the most illustrious team at that time. Hence the Hotspurs' alternate nickname: the Lilywhites.

4
GLOBAL HONOURS
1 UEFA Cup Winners' Cup
3 UEFA Europa Leagues

21
NATIONAL HONOURS
2 English Leagues
8 FA Cups
4 League Cups
7 Community Shields

2019
Champions League–
runners-up jersey

From "Lilywhites" to "Lilywinners"

The fans of Tottenham Hotspur affectionately call their club "The Lilywhites," after the team's white strip. Two years after becoming the first team in England to pull off the League–FA Cup double, Tottenham was also the first club in the country to win a European Cup, in 1963 (5–1 against Atlético de Madrid in the final of the Cup Winners' Cup). They added two more in 1972 and 1984 (UEFA Cup, ancestor of the Europa League).

Sadly, the North London team would not taste cross-Channel glory again for over forty years. At best, Spurs might console themselves with a bit of domestic silverware: one FA Cup (1991) and two League Cups (1999 and 2008). In 2019, the Lilywhites qualified for their very first Champions League final, thanks largely to their star striker Harry Kane and their cool French goalie Hugo Lloris. But after a memorable campaign, they lost to Liverpool (0–2).

Tottenham would have to wait until their third all-English duel in six European finals to break the forty-one-year-old curse, on May 21, 2025 at the San Mamés stadium in Bilbao. An own goal by Luke Shaw, the Manchester United defender, sealed it for them (1–0) and the Lilywhites became "Lilywinners" once more. Their Australian manager, Ange Postecoglou, didn't fare so well: he was fired two weeks later.

BILBAO (SPAIN), SAN MAMES
MAY 21, 2025
Promoted to captain after the departure of Harry Kane, Heung-min Son is all smiles after winning his first trophy after ten years at Tottenham.

2026
(home)

2026
(third)

2025
(home)

2025
(away)

2023
(home)

2023
(away)

2021
(home)

2017
(away)

2017
(home)

2014
(away)

2011
(home)

2006
(home)

2006
(away)

1992
(home)

1983
(away)

1981
(home)

1980
(away)

1951
(home)

Logo, you got the look

IN 2013, A DESIRE TO GROW THE PARIS SG BRAND INTERNATIONALLY LED ITS QATARI OWNERS TO GET RID OF ALL SYMBOLS ON THE LOGO THAT MIGHT BE CONSIDERED NEGATIVE. IT WASN'T A REVOLUTION BUT A MODERNISATION.

Keen to make Paris Saint-Germain one of the biggest sports brands in the world, the club's new Qatari owners (since June 30, 2011) decided to get rid of certain symbols on the logo. Unveiled on February 22, 2013, this logo's new look was designed around two key symbols—Paris and the Eiffel Tower—and incorporated a brighter red. Since the relative youth of Paris SG (no longer PSG) was a handicap when compared with other big clubs—which dated their starts from the 1800s—its year of founding (1970) was removed. The white cradle symbolising the birth of King Louis XIV in the outer Paris suburb of Saint-Germain-en-Laye, while the "Saint-Germain" part (considered confusing) was detached from the word "Paris" and placed at the bottom in smaller lettering. Only the fleur-de-lis—representing royalty and purity—was retained and gilded, although, like the Eiffel Tower, it has sometimes been replaced by the Jumpman logo, ever since Paris SG signed an exclusive three-year partnership (on September 13, 20018) with Jordan Brand, subsidiary of the American sports equipment and clothing company Nike. Paris SG's current slogan, "Revons plus grand," (Dream Bigger) is a riff on Nike's famous "Dream Big."

Logo
from 1970 to 1972

Logo
from 1992 to 1996

Logo
from 2002 to 2013

3

GLOBAL HONOURS

1 UEFA Champions League
1 UEFA Cup Winners' Cup
1 UEFA Super Cup

51

NATIONAL HONOURS

13 French Leagues
16 French Cups
9 French League Cups
13 French Super Cups

On the jersey:

Paris Saint-Germain - Atlético de Madrid
15 June 2025 - Pasadena, California
United States of America

QATAR
AIRWAYS

2025
Club World Cup jersey
for the match against
Atlético de Madrid
(4−0)

Qatar's lucky star

Paris Saint-Germain had only just won its first Champions League (4–0, against Inter Milan, on May 31, 2025) when the question of whether it would put a star on its shirt divided both fans and directors alike. Amid the excitement that this historic victory generated, the PSG marketing department rushed out a collector's shirt bearing a stylised star incorporating the shape of the Eiffel Tower. Not long after, the club unveiled their shirt for the 2025–2026 season. It also paid homage to the Eiffel Tower by depicting its metal structure within the central vertical red "Hechter" strip, named after the fashion designer and former president of the club (June 9, 1974, to January 6, 1978). But without a star. PSG wore the shirt during the Club World Cup in the United States, mainly to make an impression at an international competition.

UEFA's regulations say nothing about a star. Each club is free to decide as it wishes. The big European clubs—such as Real Madrid (fifteen Champions Leagues), AC Milan (seven), and Bayern Munich and Liverpool (six each)—don't display one. Of the twenty-three clubs that won the Champions League before Paris Saint-Germain, only Marseille, Celtic, Nottingham Forest, and Aston Villa have put a star on their shirts.

To make everyone happy, the PSG management opted for a compromise: its players would only wear the Champions League winner's star in matches played in that competition. Star or not, Paris Saint-Germain sold more than a million shirts in 2025 for the seventh season in a row.

MUNICH (GERMANY), ALLIANZ ARENA
MAY 31, 2025
Marquinhos becomes the first captain of Paris Saint-Germain to lift the Champions League trophy.

WINNERS

UEFA CHAMPIONS LEAGUE FINAL 2025

2026

(away)

2024

(home)

2023

(away)

2021

(home)

2021

(away)

2020

(home)

2020

(away)

2019

(home)

2016

(home)

2014
(home)

2014
(away)

2007
(away)

2006
(home)

1998
(away)

1995
(home)

1985
(home)

1977
(home)

1975
(away)

A working man's jersey

BORUSSIA DORTMUND, SCHALKE 04'S GREAT RUHR RIVALS, CAN TRACE THEIR ROOTS BACK TO THE WORLD OF STEELWORKERS AND MINERS, AND THEIR COLOURS ARE A REMINDER OF THAT HERITAGE.

The group of local steelworkers and miners were so excited to have established the club on December 19, 1909, they forgot to give it a name. Busy clinking overflowing glasses by that point, they decided to call it "Borussia," the name of their favourite beer (Borussia also means "Prussian" in Latin). And so the Ballspielverein ("Ball game") Borussia 1909 Dortmund was born. After starting out in blue and white, BVB 09 (as it was renamed in 1945) later adopted yellow and black—yellow for the overalls worn by its workmen supporters, and black as a tribute to its miner fans. These colours proved to be charmed as, prior to becoming the third German club to hoist the Champions League trophy in 1997 (after Bayern Munich and Hamburg), they were the first to secure European silverware on May 5, 1966 (European Cup Winners' Cup, 2–1 a.e.t. over Liverpool). They were also the first German outfit to be floated on the stock exchange in 2000. After flirting with financial ruin five years later, Die Schwarzgelben ("Black and yellows") fought back in style to land a German League and Cup double in 2012.

3
GLOBAL HONOURS
1 UEFA Champions League
1 UEFA Cup Winners' Cup
1 Intercontinental Cup

19
NATIONAL HONOURS
8 German Leagues
5 German Cups
6 German Super Cups

2012
Double–winning jersey
(German League and
German Cup)

Pierre-Emerick Aubameyang, a very striking 17

Pierre-Emerick Aubameyang has always juggled with numbers, starting with those printed on the back of his shirt. A number 9 by position, he has rarely worn it in clubs, starting out with number 41 at AC Milan, number 10 at Marseille and at Al-Qadsiah in Saudi Arabia. He only took on number 9 when he was capped for Gabon, as well as during his single season at Chelsea (2022–2023).

One of his numbers is more striking than the others: number 17. He wore it during his five years at Borussia Dortmund (2013–2018), a period that enabled this acrobatic player to make history at the Ruhr club. On August 12, 2017, the Gabonese international—already voted best player in the Bundesliga for the 2015–2016 season—scored a hat trick in the first round of the German Cup against Rielasingen-Arlen (5–0), becoming the top foreign scorer in Borussia's history, with 124 goals. Having unseated the Swiss striker Stéphane Chapuisat (123 goals from 1991 to 1999), Aubameyang consolidated his record, scoring a total of 141 in 213 matches, plus 36 decisive passes.

On January 31, 2018, he left for Arsenal, where he took Thierry Henry's number 14 for five years. He may not have had time to become the highest scorer in the history of the BVB—that title belongs to the German Adi Preissler (177 goals)—but the winner of the German Cup and top scorer of the Bundesliga (31 goals) in 2017 was a very striking number 17.

DORTMUND (GERMANY), SIGNAL IDUNA PARK
APRIL 4, 2015
Aubameyang was closely marked by the defending champions of the Bundesliga, such as Dante, during a Borussia Dortmund–Bayern Munich match (0–1).

2026
(home)

2023
(away)

2023
(home)

2018
(home)

2017
(third)

2017
(home)

2015
(home)

2015
(away)

2013
(home)

2009
(home)

2009
(away)

2007
(home)

2002
(home)

2002
(away)

2001
(away)

1983
(home)

1977
(home)

1910
(home)

Victory in white sleeves

FOUNDED ON MAY 1, 1886, THE CLUB WITH THE MOTTO "VICTORIA CONCORDIA CRESCIT" ("VICTORY THROUGH HARMONY") HAS CHANGED ITS NAME AND SHIRT NUMEROUS TIMES.

Arsenal's initial name was Dial Square F.C. (a reference to a sundial at the factory entrance). The club was later named Royal Arsenal and Woolwich Arsenal. Relegated and on the verge of bankruptcy, the club was bought in 1910, and soon moved to the Arsenal Stadium in Highbury, North London, in 1913, whereupon it was renamed Arsenal FC. As it was the first London club to gain promotion to the First Division in 1904, club officials were unable to find appropriate jerseys in the London area. Instead, they appealed to Nottingham Forest, who sent them a supply of dark red jerseys, Forest's colour of choice at the time. Over the years, the dark red was significantly lightened, and in 1933 white sleeves were introduced for a home match against Liverpool. The change helped the team stand out against the all-red Liverpool and the now famous white sleeves have featured ever since except for two seasons between 1965 and 1967 when all-red shirts were preferred, and during the 2005–2006 season when Arsenal reverted to their original dark red colours to mark their last campaign at Highbury. Adding white to the sleeves seems to have been a wise decision as throughout the 20th century Arsenal were the best team in England with an average league position of 8.5, just ahead of all-red Liverpool.

1
GLOBAL HONOUR
1 UEFA Europa League

46
NATIONAL HONOURS
13 English Leagues
14 FA Cups
2 League Cups
17 Community Shields

2004
English League–
winning jersey

Henry, Arsenal's 12th man

Since December 10, 2011, a statue of Thierry Henry has stood outside the Emirates Stadium. It captures the Frenchman doing his traditional goal celebration.

And suddenly, as if by magic, the statue erected in Thierry Henry's honour on December 10, 2011 on the Emirates Stadium forecourt came to life. The French forward climbed down from his pedestal to take to the pitch and score once again for Arsenal. The turn of events cost British bookmakers, who were not convinced by the comeback, the princely sum of €1.2 million. "Titi is a legend here. He left an unforgettable imprint on the history of the club. His goal only serves to further enhance his reputation," said a delighted Arsène Wenger at the time. When his former protégé (1999–2007) came back to Arsenal to keep himself fit during the MLS off-season, the experienced coach offered him a six-week contract. "It was difficult for me to say no," explained the New York Red Bulls front-man, voted greatest Arsenal player of all time and best foreign player to ever grace the Premier League in 2008. Henry wore the number 14 jersey in his first spell with Arsenal, but that now belonged to Theo Walcott. He chose 12, the number on his back when he lifted the World Cup in 1998.

It was in that number that the 35-year-old hit the back of the net against Blackburn (7–1) and Sunderland (2–1). He brought his short assignment to a close by appearing in a seventh match, a 4–0 Champions League loss in Milan on February 16, 2012. And then, the Gunners' all-time leading goalscorer (228 goals) continued on his way. His statue, on the other hand, will remain forever.

With 228 goals to his name, Thierry Henry is the Gunners' all-time top-scorer.

The players of Arsenal Women FC celebrate winning the FA Women's Super League.

Arsenal Women FC

Star Women

Founded in 1987, Arsenal Women FC today holds the most titles of any English women's club, as well as being the first and only English women's team to win the Champions League. Arsenal Women Football Club was founded in 1987 by Vic Akers (the long-term kit manager of Arsenal's men's team). He managed the club for twenty-two years before becoming its honorary president. The ladies took their first major title, the FA Women's National League Cup, in 1992, the year in which they also gained promotion to the FA Women's Premier League. The club turned professional in 2004, and moved to Meadow Park, where they shared the pitches with the boys of Boreham Wood FC, in Hertfordshire, to the north of London. Incidentally, the town of Bore-hamwood has been nicknamed the "British Hollywood," owing to the several film studios that have been based there over the decades. Among the productions shot there were several of the *Indiana Jones* and *Star Wars* films. The legend that is Arsenal Women (holder of the most titles of any English women's club) was written by stars such as English striker Marieanne Spacey-Cale (1993–2002), English defender Faye White (1996–2013), and the Irish goalie Emma Byrne (2000–16). In 2007, the club became the first British winner of the UEFA Women's Champions League.

2026
(home)

2026
(away)

2025
(home)

2024
(away)

2023
(home)

2023
(third)

2022
(home)

2021
(away)

2019
(home)

2017
(home)

2017
(away)

2013
(home)

2006
(home)

2005
(away)

2003
(home)

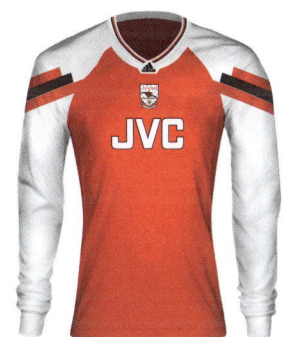

1994
(home)

1932
(home)

1906
(home)

Straight for goal

FOLLOWING THE MOTTO INSCRIBED ON THEIR CLUB CREST TO THE LETTER, MARSEILLE INCREASED THE PROFILE OF THEIR JERSEY BY PLAYING AN EFFECTIVE STYLE THAT TOOK FRANCE AND EUROPE BY STORM.

The details of the foundation of Olympique de Marseille are as murky as a bowl of bouillabaisse, the fish stew that originated in the southern French city. Some believe the club was founded in August 1899 by way of a merger between the fencing club "L'Epée" and the "Football Club de Marseille," who are said to have bequeathed the famous "Droit au but" ("Straight for goal") motto, which adorned the badge up until 1935 and then again after 1986. For others, l'OM, officially recognised by law on December 12, 1900, was formed in 1892. The club itself has opted for 1899. The colour white was adopted right from the start as a nod towards the purity of the Olympian ideal extolled by Pierre de Coubertin—all of the athletes at the first modern Olympic Games, held in Athens in 1896, were dressed in white. Marseille have constantly changed both their away and third colours ever since the return of Adidas as kit supplier in 1974 (Adidas was replaced by Reebok and Mizuno from 1994 to 1996, and again by Puma since 1 July 2018). Despite marketing concerns, the home top kept its original white. It also boasts a gold star above the crest, which was added in 1993 to mark Marseille's historic Champions League victory. To date, they remain the only French side to have won Europe's premier club tournament.

DROIT AU BUT

1

GLOBAL HONOUR

1 UEFA Champions League

25

NATIONAL HONOURS

9 French Leagues
10 French Cups
3 French League Cups
3 French Super Cups

1993
Champions League–
winning jersey

Papin's benevolent streak

A Bordeaux-based friend of Jean-Pierre Papin broke down in tears the day the French striker gave him a case full of jerseys as a present. "I had about 60 of them, including some old Soviet and Yugoslav ones," recalls the 1991 European Footballer of the Year. "I knew he collected football jerseys, and I preferred to see them framed on his wall rather than get eaten by moths," he continues. Papin demonstrated the same type of generosity throughout his career. "The whole point of a jersey is to provide people with pleasure. Players should hand out ten a day to supporters who don't have enough money to buy one. That's what I did, to the extent that people—who I often don't remember giving anything to—still come up to me today to show me them," says the former France international. The five-time French League top goalscorer (1988–1992) did keep one jersey for himself, the one he wore when bidding farewell to Marseille supporters at the Stade Vélodrome on April 25, 1992, a match in which the home side defeated Cannes 2–0. "It's symbolic; in fact, I kept one jersey from six of the clubs I played for, Valenciennes, Bruges, Marseille, Milan, Bayern Munich and Bordeaux. A lack of space means I don't have one from my last club, Guingamp (1998), because I had them transformed into chairs by Laurent Pardo, a French designer. The jerseys were used to upholster the chairs, which I've arranged around the poker table in my house in Arcachon. The only thing I collect is balls. I've got some made of glass, wood, leather and, of course, one made of gold: my Ballon d'Or European Footballer of the Year award. That sits on the living room table, because I want to see it every day!" he concludes with a smile.

Jean-Pierre Papin's acrobatic volleys gave birth to a new French footballing term: "Papinade."

2026
(away)

2026
(home)

2025
(away)

2025
(third)

2023
(home)

2023
(third)

2020
(fourth)

2017
(home)

2012
(third)

2010
(home)

2009
(away)

2005
(home)

2004
(third)

2001
(home)

1999
(third)

1985
(home)

1980
(away)

1972
(home)

In the pink

CO-OWNED BY DAVID BECKHAM, INTER MIAMI CF (FOUNDED ON JANUARY 29, 2018) HAS CHOSEN TO PLAY IN PINK AS A NOD TO THE SOUL OF SOUTHERN FLORIDA.

On September 5, 2018, a little over eight months after its official founding, Club Internacional de Fùtbol Miami (or Inter Miami CF for short) unveiled its strip, opting for a white and pink colour scheme, which became entirely pink from the 2022–2023 season (black for away matches). This bright colour reflects the vibrant soul of Southern Florida and embodies the audacious spirit of the club and its fans from the first season of the twenty-fifth franchise of Major League Soccer (MLS) in 2020.

Designed in a style and colours recalling the city's Art Deco character, the badge depicts two large white herons at its centre, with pink highlights. Their intertwined legs form a letter "M" for Miami. Between the herons is an eclipse with seven sunrays, in homage to the famous number worn by the club's co-founder and president David Beckham when he was a player. The club's name runs around the edge of the badge, with the Roman numerals MMXX standing for the first season (2020) of Florida's second club in MLS (after Orlando City Soccer Club).

1

GLOBAL HONOUR

1 Leagues Cup

1

NATIONAL HONOUR

1 Supporters' Shield

2024
Leagues Cup-winning jersey

2026
(home)

2026
Jersey worn during the FIFA Club World Cup

2025
Supporters' Shield-winning jersey

2025
(home)

Old friends

Having moved to Florida, and with his Barcelona days behind him, Lionel Messi was still able to reconnect with his past. Six days after his official arrival at Inter Miami, on July 15, 2023, the captain of the 2022 World Champions played his first match with the Herons under coach Gerardo "Tata" Martino who, in addition to being a fellow Rosario native, was also Messi's manager at Barça (2013–2014) and then the Albiceleste (2014–2016).

"Tata" left on November 20, 2024 for "personal reasons," but Messi could still count on some Barça buddies. Sergio Busquets signed for Inter Miami the day after Messi's arrival, and Jordi Alba five days later. On August 19, Inter Miami took its very first trophy, beating Nashville SC (1–1, 10–9 on penalties) in the final of the Leagues Cup—for which the 47 teams of the MLS and the Liga MX (Mexican championship) compete. This victory owed much to the six-times Ballon d'Or, who scored ten goals in seven matches, including the final.

In addition to finding an ideal lifestyle for his family and continuing to win titles, "la Pulga" was also joined by Luis Suarez to share his American dream. Reuniting two-thirds of Barça's "MNS" (without Neymar) enabled Inter Miami to win its first Supporters' Shield—a trophy awarded each year to the team having won the most points during the regular season. Striker of the splendid winning free kick against Porto (2–1), Suarez then helped Miami into the last sixteen of the Club World Cup against PSG (0–4) on June 29, 2025. Javier Mascherano, another veteran of Barça (2010–2018) and Argentina, succeeded Tata Martino as manager, so continuing Messi's reunion with old friends in the United States.

FORT LAUDERDALE (UNITED STATES), CHASE STADIUM
MAY 4, 2025, 39TH MINUTE
Lionel Messi congratulates Luis Suarez after scoring the third of Inter Miami's four goals against the New York Red Bulls (4–1).

A grocer's smock

SAINT-ÉTIENNE IS THE ONLY FRENCH CLUB WITH A TRICOLOR STAR—SYMBOLISING ITS TEN CHAMPIONSHIP TITLES—AND IT OWES ITS GREEN COLOUR TO THE FRENCH SUPERMARKET CHAIN CASINO, WHOSE OWNER FOUNDED THE CLUB.

His bust sits proudly beside the entrance to the locker room of the stadium that bears his name, for the Association Sportive de Saint-Étienne owes everything to Geoffroy-Guichard, owner of the Casino supermarket chain, who founded the original club in 1919. Green was the colour of the shutters of his grocery stores, and the club—initially called the Amicale des Employés de la Société des Magasins Casino before adopting its current name in 1927 and turning professional in 1933—has always played with this colour. But it took the spread of colour television in the 1970s—a period when Saint-Étienne was setting European football alight—for the club to become known as Les Verts (the Greens). Along with the Reds of Liverpool, Saint-Étienne remains one of the few teams known throughout the world for the colour of its strip. In 1968, the club adopted the black panther as its emblem (following a competition involving the Saint-Étienne art school, in homage to their Malian striker Salif Keïta, who was awarded the first ever Ballon d'Or Africain, in 1970. The panther has now disappeared from the club's badge, but since 1993, it has been surmounted by a tricolour star (blue, white, and red) in honour of AS Saint-Étienne being the first club to have won ten French championship titles.

0
GLOBAL HONOUR

17
NATIONAL HONOURS
10 French Leagues
6 French Cups
1 French League Cups

Cheeky Spider-Man

Jérémie Janot had prepared his stunt well. Already wearing a Spider-Man shirt, he waited until the team posed for the official photo of the AS Saint-Étienne versus FC Istres game (2–0) on May 21, 2005, before pulling the Spider-Man mask from his shorts and putting it on, to the general surprise of everyone there. "Then I ran across the pitch and only took it off once I was in my goal. The craziest thing was the way the stadium just exploded that day," said the Saint-Étienne goalkeeper. The image went around the world. But Janot had previous history as a prankster. With the support of regional sportswear firm Duarig, Janot had often worn a special handmade shirt for big occasions. "During one derby, I taunted the Brazilians of Lyon by wearing an Argentina shirt," he said. Other outings saw him dressed in military camouflage, a paintball outfit, the Pink Panther, the polka-dotted King of the Mountains jersey from the Tour de France (in homage to Richard Virenque), and that of the Paris rugby team Stade Français in Marseille (Paris SG's big rival). "But after reaching a peak with Spider-Man, we didn't want to fall into stupid or ridiculous one-upmanship, and end up doing one outfit too many. So that's why we stopped, just before Darth Vader!"

Pierre-Emerick Aubameyang, a fan of Marvel superheroes, picked up the torch by putting on a Spider-Man mask too, in celebration of his goal on October 26, 2012, when Saint-Étienne played Stade Rennes (2-0). At Arsenal, he took out a Black Panther mask (again when playing Rennes) in the quarterfinal return leg of the UEFA Europa League (3-0), on March 14, 2019 (away leg: 1-3). He had already used others during his time at Dortmund (2013–18), which led him to join CR7 in signing a lifetime contract with Nike (in March 2017), becoming "the Masked Finisher."

At Borussia Dortmund, Pierre-Emerick Aubameyang imitated Jérémie Janot, his former goalie at Saint-Étienne.

2026
(home)

2023
(third)

2022
(home)

2021
(home)

2018
(away)

2017
(home)

2015
(away)

2013
(French Cup)

2013
(away)

2012
(home)

2010
(away)

2009
(home)

1987
(home)

1985
(home)

1984
(away)

1974-1978
(home)

1957
(home)

1933
(home)

Hungry like lionesses

LYON'S WOMEN'S FOOTBALL TEAM WAS SOLD TO AMERICAN BUSINESSWOMAN MICHELE KANG ON MAY 16, 2023. SHE RENAMED IT "OL LYONNES" IN 2025.

Lyon has had a women's football team since 1970—as a part of the FC Lyon sports club—and had taken four French championship titles (1991, 1993, 1995, and 1998), but it had to wait until the summer of 2004 to officially become part of Olympique Lyonnais. Three years later Lyon pulled off a record men's-women's double. For the first time in France, the same club was champion of both the men's and the women's first division. Olympique Lyonnais FC went one better in 2008, when the women's side won their first double (French cup and French championship)—that is to say, exactly the same as the men's side. The club's success attracted the attention of the American businesswoman, Michele Kang, a Palm Beach friend and neighbour of John Textor (who acquired the OL Groupe on December 19, 2022). On May 16, 2023, Kang bought a 52% stake in OL Féminin. The remaining 48% (valued at nearly $58M) remained in the ownership of the OL Groupe. Nearly two years later, the women's club was renamed "OL Lyonnes," and on May 19, 2025 it received a new logo. The club is now twinned with the Washington Spirit and London City Lionesses franchises, also owned by YMK Holdings.

8
GLOBAL HONOURS
8 UEFA Women's Champions Leagues

31
NATIONAL HONOURS
18 Women's French Leagues
10 Women's French Cups
3 Trophées des championnes

2019
UEFA Women's Champions League- winning jersey

Hegerberg, forever first

The Norwegian international Ada Hegerberg was only twenty-three years old when she walked up the steps to the Grand Palais in Paris (on December 3, 2018) in a gold dress to pick up the first ever women's Ballon d'Or. Six months earlier, Olympique Lyonnais FC, her club since 2014, had already showered her in silver, so to speak, offering her the highest-ever contract in the history of women's football (between $440,000 (€400,000) and $550,000 (€500,000) gross a year) in exchange for extending her contract until June 30, 2021.

Hegerberg's talent is priceless. When she won the Ballon d'Or, this unmatched goal scorer had already notched up an incredible record of 185 goals in 149 matches, played while wearing the Lyon shirt, including an astounding hat trick in sixteen minutes flat during the final of the UEFA Women's Champions League against FC Barcelona Women (4–1, May 18, 2019). She was the first woman to pull off such a feat in a UWCL final, to the great joy of her sister, Andrine—two years her elder—against whom she used to play when Andrine was a midfielder for Paris SG (2018–19). Yes, football is a family affair for the Hegerbergs: their father, Stein Erik, was a midfielder before turning to coaching, while their mother, Gerd, was an international striker. Ada Hegerberg has been in a relationship with Thomas Rogne—another Norwegian international, and a centre-back—since 2016 (they married in May 2019).

LYON (FRANCE), GROUPAMA STADIUM
DECEMBER 5, 2018
Ada Hegerberg shows off her Ballon d'Or at the Lyon's men's team's League One match against Stade Rennes (0–2).

2026
(home)

2026
(away)

2025
(third)

2024
(home)

2024
(third)

2013
(home)

2023
(away)

2021
(away)

2018
(home)

2018
(away)

2017
(home)

2017
(away)

2016
(away)

2014
(home)

2012
(away)

2011
(away)

2008
(home)

2005
(home)

The devourers devoured

FFC FRANKFURT HAS BEEN ONE OF THE BASTIONS OF EUROPEAN WOMEN'S FOOTBALL, ALONG WITH OLYMPIQUE LYONNAIS FC, BUT THEY RECENTLY AGREED TO JOIN EINTRACHT FRANKFURT (A MEN'S TEAM), STARTING WITH THE 2020–21 SEASON.

Women's football was first played in Frankfurt in 1973, but it was not until August 27, 1998, that Frauen-Fußball-Club Frankfurt was born—a female player takes pride of place in the centre of its logo. 1. FFC Frankfurt has fiercely cherished its status as an independent women's football club for many years. Indeed, with twenty titles in two decades, including four UEFA Women's Champions League titles from six finals, it is Germany's most successful women's football club, and Europe's second—behind Olympique Lyonnais Féminin. However, its recent decline ended up convincing its directors of the necessity of joining the men's team. In June 2020, 1. FFC Frankfurt is absorbed into Eintracht Frankfurt, a club in the Bundesliga. "We are extremely happy that the Eintracht management decided to forge a joint future," Siegfried Dietrich (the manager of 1. FFC Frankfurt) says happily. "It is now up to us to support our members, our fans and our sponsors on this new path." However, the Frankfurt female players did not win any titles in the 2015-2025 decade.

4
GLOBAL HONOURS
4 UEFA Women's Champions Leagues

16
NATIONAL HONOURS
7 Women's German Leagues
9 Women's German Cups

2015
UEFA Women's
Champions League-
winning jersey

1999
Double winning jersey
(German League
and German Cup)

2001
Women's German
League-
winning jersey

2006
UEFA Women's
Champions League-
winning jersey

2014
Women's German
Cup-winning jersey

The Other Clásico

EVER SINCE THE CREATION OF A REAL MADRID WOMEN'S TEAM IN 2020, SPAIN HAS MARCHED TO THE BEAT OF A SECOND CLÁSICO—ONE DOMINATED BY BARÇA, THE NEW BASTION OF WOMEN'S FOOTBALL IN EUROPE.

The FC Barcelona women's team won the first Clásico 4–0 on October 4, 2020, and the next seventeen as well, before their first defeat, on March 23, 2025 (1–3). This clash of titans has been insanely popular. On March 30, 2022, Camp Nou hosted 91,553 spectators for a Barcelona–Real match in the Champions League, setting a world record that was beaten just weeks later, on April 22, when Barça played Wolfsburg at home, also in the Champions League (91,648 spectators). This was a larger crowd than even the highest attendance for a Women's World Cup: 90,185 spectators at the USA–China final at the Rose Bowl, Pasadena on July 10, 1999 (0–0, 5–4 on penalties).

FC Barcelona Femení became an official section of FC Barcelona in 2001 (the year the Superliga was established) and reached its first Champions League final in 2019, going on to play five of the following six finals, winning three. The Barça girls have come a long way from their first match: a Christmas charity game in 1970.

3
GLOBAL HONOURS
3 UEFA Women's Champions Leagues

26
NATIONAL HONOURS
10 Spanish Leagues
11 Spanish Cups
5 Spanish Super Cups

2025
UEFA Women's Champions League-winning jersey

2023
(home)

2022
(away)

2020
(home)

2019
(home)

Appendix

Paris Saint-Germain (France)
"Je suis Paris"
(November 2015)

AS Saint-Étienne (France)
"Pray for Paris"
(November 2015)

Hamilton Academical (Scotland)
Homage to the victims of the Paris attacks
(November 2015)

OGC Nice (France)
"Heart" shirt
(August 2016)

Serie A (Italy)
"Genoa in our hearts"
(August 2018)

RC Strasbourg (France)
"Strasbourg, mon amour"
(December 2018)

Paris Saint-Germain (France)
"Notre-Dame"
(April 2019)

FC Barcelona (Spain)
"Gràcies Johan"
(April 2016)

Corinthians (Brazil)
"Magic Senna"
(October 2018)

Bohemian FC (Ireland)
"Bob Marley"
(October 2018)

Juventus FC (Italy)
1997 (centenary)

Olympique de Marseille (France)
1998 (centenary)

FC Barcelona (Spain)
1999 (centenary)

Arsenal (England)
2006 (Highbury, 1913-2006)

Inter Milan (Italy)
2008 (centenary)

Corinthians (Brazil)
2010 (centenary)

Lazio (Italy)
2010
(110 years, third)

Paris-SG (France)
2011 (40 years)

Fluminense (Brazil)
2012 (110 years)

Santos (Brazil)
2012
(centenary, third)

Celtic FC (Scotland)
2013
(125 years, third)

Genoa (Italy)
2013
(centenary, away)

United States (national team)
2013 (centenary)

PSV Eindhoven (Netherlands)
2014
(centenary, away)

Manchester City (England)
2019 (125 years)

**Colorado Caribous
(United States)**
1978

Ajax Amsterdam (Netherlands)
1990 (away)

Australia (national team)
1991

**Manchester United
(England)**
1991 (away)

Arsenal (England)
1992 (away)

**Queens Park Rangers
(England)**
1992 (goalkeeper)

Reading (England)
1992 (away)

Atalanta Bergamo (Italy)
1994 (away)

Bristol Rovers (England)
1994 (away)

Derby County (England)
1994 (away)

Hull City (England)
1994

Madureira (Brazil)
1994

Shamrock Rovers (Ireland)
1994 (away)

Chelsea FC (England)
1995 (away)

Notts County (England)
1995 (away)

Scunthorpe United (England)
1995 (away)

Croatia (national team)
1996 (goalkeeper)

England (national team)
1996 (goalkeeper)

FC Barcelona (Spain)
1997 (away)

Manchester United (England)
1998 (goalkeeper)

Mexico (national team)
1998

Bochum (Germany)
1998

Mexico (national team)
1999 (goalkeeper)

Jaguares de Chiapas (Mexico)
2003

Athletic Bilbao (Spain)
2004

AS Saint-Étienne (France)
2005 (goalkeeper)

Olympique de Marseille (France)
2012 (third)

Olympique Lyonnais (France)
2011 (away)

Everton (England)
2012 (goalkeeper)

Charleroi SC (Belgium)
2013

Recreativo de Huelva (Spain)
2013 (away)

FC Rostov (Russia)
2019 (fourth)

SC Braga (Portugal)
2020 (third)

so vintage

jerseys from days of old

Juventus FC (Italy)
1898

Chelsea FC (England)
1905

Boca Juniors (Argentina)
1907

Santos (Brazil)
1912

Flamengo (Brazil)
1915

Pénarol (Uruguay)
1920

Torino FC (Italy)
1949

Fluminense (Brazil)
1940

Monterrey (Mexico)
1945

Vélez Sarsfield (Argentina)
1945

South Africa (national team)
1947

Jamaica (national team)
1948

Spain (national team)
1950

United States (national team)
1950

Dukla Prague (Czechoslovakia)
1960

AS Monaco (France)
1961

Cuba (national team)
1962

AS Roma (Italy)
1966

Celtic Glasgow (Scotland)
1967

Congo (national team)
1968

Parma (Italy)
1969

SSD Palermo (Italy)
1970 (away)

Albania (national team)
1973

GDR (national team)
1974

Japan (national team)
1974

Netherlands (national team)
1974

Zaïre (national team)
1974

Los Angeles Aztecs (United States)
1976

Northern Ireland (national team)
1977

SC Bastia (France)
1978

Chemnitzer FC (Germany)
1978

Guatemala (national team)
1978

Tampa Bay Rowdies (United States)
1978

**Fort Lauderdale Strikers
(United States)**
1979

**New England Tea Men
(United States)**
1979

**California Surf
(United States)**
1980 (away)

Ghana (national team)
1980

Mali (national team)
1980

**Mozambique
(national team)**
1980

Suriname (national team)
1980

Montreal Manic (Canada)
1981

Mexico (national team)
1982 (away)

Girondins de Bordeaux (France)
1960

Lyon (France)
1963

Nantes (France)
1966

North Korea (national team)
1966 (away)

Rangers FC (Scotland)
1972

Dynamo Kiev (Ukraine)
1975

West Ham (England)
1977

Peru (national team)
1978

Nantes (France)
1979

Ballon d'Or jerseys

covered in glory by heroes

1956
Stanley Matthews
Blackpool

1957
Alfredo Di Stéfano
Real Madrid

1958
Raymond Kopa
Real Madrid

1959
Alfredo Di Stéfano
Real Madrid

1960
Luis Suarez
FC Barcelona

1961
Omar Sivori
Juventus FC

1962
Josef Masopust
Dukla Prague

1963
Lev Yachine
Dynamo Moscow

1964
Denis Law
Manchester United

1965
Eusébio
SL Benfica

1966
Bobby Charlton
Manchester United

1967
Florian Albert
Ferencváros TC

1968
George Best
Manchester United

1969
Gianni Rivera
AC Milan

1970
Gerd Muller
Bayern Munich

1971
Johan Cruyff
Ajax Amsterdam

1972
Franz Beckenbauer
Bayern Munich

1973
Johan Cruyff
FC Barcelona

1974
Johan Cruyff
FC Barcelona

1975
Oleg Blokhine
FC Dynamo Kyiv

1976
Franz Beckenbauer
Bayern Munich

1977
Allan Simonsen
Borussia
Mönchengladbach

1978
Kevin Keegan
Hamburger SV

1979
Kevin Keegan
Hamburger SV

1980
Karl-Heinz Rummenigge
Bayern Munich

1981
Karl-Heinz Rummenigge
Bayern Munich

1982
Paolo Rossi
Juventus FC

1983
Michel Platini
Juventus FC

1984
Michel Platini
Juventus FC

1985
Michel Platini
Juventus FC

1986
IgorBelanov
FC Dynamo Kyiv

1987
Ruud Gullit
AC Milan

1988
Marco Van Basten
AC Milan

1989
Marco Van Basten
AC Milan

1990
Lothar Matthaus
Inter Milan

1991
Jean-Pierre Papin
Olympique de Marseille

1992
Marco Van Basten
AC Milan

1993
Roberto Baggio
Juventus FC

1994
Hristo Stoichkov
FC Barcelona

1995
George Weah
AC Milan

1996
Matthias Sammer
Borussia Dortmund

1997
Ronaldo
Inter Milan

1998
Zinédine Zidane
Juventus FC

1999
Rivaldo
FC Barcelona

2000
Luis Figo
Real Madrid

2001
Michael Owen
Liverpool FC

2002
Cristiano Ronaldo
Real Madrid

2003
Pavel Nedved
Juventus FC

2004
Andrei Shevchenko
AC Milan

2005
Ronaldinho
FC Barcelona

2006
Fabio Cannavaro
Real Madrid

2007
Kaká
AC Milan

2008
Ronaldo
Manchester United

2009
Lionel Messi
FC Barcelona

2010
Lionel Messi
FC Barcelona

2011
Lionel Messi
FC Barcelona

2012
Lionel Messi
FC Barcelona

2013
Cristiano Ronaldo
Real Madrid

2014
Cristiano Ronaldo
Real Madrid

2015
Lionel Messi
FC Barcelona

2016
Cristiano Ronaldo
Real Madrid

2017
Cristiano Ronaldo
Real Madrid

2018
Luka Modrić
Real Madrid

2019
Lionel Messi
FC Barcelona

2021
Lionel Messi
Paris Saint-Germain

2022
Karim Benzema
Real Madrid

2023
Lionel Messi
Paris Saint-Germain

2024
Rodri
Manchester City

2025
Ousmane Dembélé
Paris Saint-Germain